The NCEA *Catholic Educational Leadership*
Monograph Series

Architects of Catholic Culture:

Designing & Building Catholic Culture in Catholic Schools

Timothy J. Cook

National Catholic Educational Association

Published in the United States of America by

The National Catholic Educational Association
1005 Glebe Road Suite 525
Arlington, VA 22201
Copyright 2001
ISBN 1-55833-255-3
Part No. ADM-20-1244
Seventh Printing, 2013

Richard M. Jacobs, O.S.A., Editor
Daniel F. Curtin, Series Supervisor

Production by Phyllis Kokus
Design by Beatriz Ruiz

Printed in the United States of America

Table of Contents

Series Introduction   v

Editor's Preface   xv

Introduction   1

Chapter 1
Organizational culture and its origins   5

Chapter 2
Catholic school culture   11

Chapter 3
Core beliefs and values   17

Chapter 4
Heroes and heroines   31

Chapter 5
Symbols   39

Chapter 6
Ritual tradition   47

Chapter 7
Human communication   59

Chapter 8
History   71

Chapter 9
Cultural players   83

Chapter 10
Architects of Catholic Culture:
Seven norms for Catholic educational leaders   95

References   103

NCEA *Catholic Educational Leadership* Monograph Series:

Authority and Decision Making in Catholic Schools

Architects of Catholic Culture: Designing & Building Catholic Culture in Catholic Schools

Character and the Contemplative Principal

The Grammar of Catholic Schooling

The Vocation of the Catholic Educator

The NCEA's Catholic Educational Leadership monograph series provides Catholic educational leaders access to literature integrating Catholic educational philosophy, theology, and history with the best available educational leadership theory and practice. Each volume is intended primarily for aspiring and practicing principals, as well as for graduate students in Catholic educational leadership programs, superintendents, pastors and seminarians, and also for Catholic educators and parents, as well as members of Catholic school boards.

Editor:

Richard M. Jacobs, O.S.A.
Villanova University

Series Supervisor:

Daniel F. Curtin
National Catholic Educational Association

Series Introduction

The NCEA's Catholic Educational Leadership Monograph Series: Reflective Guides for Catholic Educational Leaders

• The principal's importance...

Research studying the principalship reveals just how important principals are in fostering school improvement (Griffiths, 1988; Murphy, 1990, 1992; Smylie & Brownlee-Conyers, 1992). Although the place where much of the action in schools transpires is in its classrooms (and hence, educational reformers focus largely upon what transpires in the teaching/learning context), much of the school's success seems to hinge largely upon the principal's ability to make sense of things in such a way that teachers become more effective in accomplishing in their classrooms what they are there to accomplish (Ackerman, Donaldson, & van der Bogert, 1996).

Perhaps principals figure so prominently in efforts to improve schooling because role expectations and personalities interact in a very powerful way, as Getzels and Guba (1957) argued nearly four decades ago. Or perhaps this effect is due simply to the eminence of the principal's office, given its focal prominence—not only from an architectural perspective but also from a psychological perspective. While researchers suggest that principals do influence and shape life within schools in ways that no other single role, personality, or office can (Beck & Murphy, 1992), researchers are not at all unanimous about the conditions that make this so, as Foster (1980a, 1980b) so astutely observes.

Whatever the actual reason may be, principals do occupy an important role, one vesting them with authority to articulate the school's fundamental purpose to a variety of constituents. In Catholic schools, principals may articulate this purpose at the opening liturgy of the school year and at the back-to-school night, pronouncing for all to hear "who we are," "what we shall be about," and, "the way we do things around here." Principals also reiterate their school's fundamental purpose while admonishing students or offering professional advice and counsel to their teachers. In the midst of a tragedy (for example, the death of a teacher, of a student's parent or pet, or as sadly is becoming all too frequent today, the violent and senseless death of a youngster), it is the principal who is expected to utter words of consolation on behalf of the entire school community. In these and many other situations, the principal's words can give deeper meaning to actions and events in terms of the school's purpose.

When principals effectively marshal the resources of their role, personalities, and office in leading others to share the school's purpose, teachers and students, for example, can direct their efforts toward achieving the school's goals. It is this synergy of efforts, Vaill (1986) argues, that sets "high performing systems" apart from mediocre or even good organizations. "Purposing," as Vaill describes this synergy, is that "stream of leadership activities which induce in the organization's membership clarity and consensus about the organization's fundamental beliefs, goals, and aspirations" (p. 91).

Without doubt, there are many Catholic school principals who capably articulate their school's purpose. In addition, these principals deftly manage what it means to be a member of the school community. In sum, these principals make it possible for others to identify their self-interest with the school's purpose.

• A threat to the school's Catholic identity...

For well over a century, religious women and men and priests have engaged in *Catholic* educational purposing, making it possible for generations of teachers and students to contribute to and experience great satisfaction and outstanding achievement as they have directed their efforts to fulfilling their school's Catholic purpose. For many teachers and students, the devotion of the religious sisters and brothers and priests inspired them to such an extent that the Catholic school's identity became identified with the selfless devotion of these men and women (Jacobs, 1998a, 1998b, 1998c). And, rightly so.

However, in the decades following the close of the Second Vatican Council, the number of religious sisters and brothers and priests steadily declined. Meanwhile, the percentage of lay men and women who have committed themselves to the Church's educational apostolate increased markedly, although the total pool of Catholic schools (and hence, of teachers and principals) declined overall. While these trends indicate that some laity are generously responding to God's call to serve as educators in Catholic schools, as with all changes, new threats and opportunities emerge.

The exodus of religious sisters and brothers and priests from Catholic schools, however, is not the most significant issue that must be reckoned with. The paramount issue posed by this exodus concerns how the laity will receive the formation they need in order to preserve and perfect the identity of the Catholic school. If lay principals are to lead their school communities to engage in Catholic educational purposing, they will need the philosophical, theological, and historical training that was part-and-parcel of the formation program for religious sisters and brothers and priests whose communities staffed Catholic schools. The formation that young religious received in prior generations, for better or worse, provided an introduction to the purpose of Catholic education, one intended to guide decision making once they would begin teaching and administering in Catholic schools. Without such a formative program, it is difficult to envision how, even though with the best of intentions, lay principals will engage in authentic Catholic educational purposing and foster their school's Catholic identity.

How, then, will the laity receive the appropriate formative training they need to teach and administer effectively in Catholic schools?

In fact, generic teacher and administrator training can be undertaken at any college or university that sponsors these programs. Typical training includes an array of courses, field experiences, and internships designed to influence how an educator will deal with the problems of practice. In most places, teacher training commences during the undergraduate years when students select education as their major. On the other hand, administrator training programs begin at the graduate level, and most programs presuppose that the aspiring administrator has attained a sufficient teaching experience to be able to develop a richer and more complex understanding about what school administration really entails. Overall, the intention behind all professional training, whether it be for teachers or administrators, is to ensure that graduates possess the fundamental skills and knowledge that will enable them to practice their craft competently.

However, competence is only a first step. There are other important matters that educators must address as part of their work in schools, not the least of which is the substantive purpose for which we educate youth.

Aware of this need, administrator preparation is changing (Murphy, 1992; Prestine & Thurston, 1994). Many programs now introduce students to the notion of educational "purposing," as Vaill (1986) describes it, seeking to foster in students a consciousness that the principal's purpose in schools embraces "focusing upon a core mission," "formulating a consensus," and "collaborating in a shared vision." But, it must be remembered, purposing is not cheerleading. Instead, purposing necessitates a leader capable of translating a vision about substantive purposes into concrete activities.

How will Catholic principals receive the training that will qualify them to translate the "grammar of Catholic schooling" (Jacobs, 1997) into actions that symbolize the abstract values embedded in the Catholic school's purpose?

- ## The principal and Catholic educational purposing...
  To bring the moral and intellectual purpose of Catholic schooling

to fruition, Catholic schools need principals who can lead their faculty and students to embrace and to be animated by the Catholic vision of life. This requirement assumes, however, that Catholic principals have received training in the philosophical and theological purposes at the heart of this apostolate.

Honed through centuries of the Church's experience, some of these philosophical and theological purposes challenge current practice, requiring educators to consider why they do what they do in their classrooms and schools. Other Catholic educational purposes flatly contradict current notions about teaching and administering schools. If Catholic educational leaders are to provide leadership in the Catholic schools entrusted to their ministry, they need to know and understand why and how Catholic educational philosophy and theology stand critical of some current educational trends while being supportive of others.

In addition to the theological and philosophical purposes at the heart of the Catholic schooling, principals of Catholic schools also need to be conversant with Catholic educational history, particularly as this drama has been enacted in the United States. The U.S. Catholic community's epic struggle to provide for the moral and intellectual formation of its youth offers Catholic principals today instructive lessons about the culture and identity of the Catholic school, its purpose and importance, as well as what educators in Catholic schools ought to be doing for students. Being conversant with the experience of the U.S. Catholic community in its attempt to educate youth will enable Catholic school principals to place the issues confronting them within a larger historical context, to see how many of the issues facing them today have been dealt with in previous generations, and to respond to these issues in concert with the lessons to be learned from the rich heritage of Catholic educational history.

Earlier this century, when religious sisters and brothers and priests predominated the landscape of Catholic schooling, parents could assume with relative certainty that the school's principal, at least, was familiar with Catholic educational theology, philosophy, and history. In most cases, principals familiar with these matters provided educational leadership steeped in Catholic educational principles. Most significantly, training provided principals a background in the purposes underlying Catholic education and, as a consequence, enabled them to speak authoritatively about the school, its programs, and its effects upon students. Ironically, it was during this era that, while most knew what the Catholic school stood for, few worried about how it was managed. In striking contrast, as politicians, policymakers, and the public worry today more and more about managing schools and link this concept to quality education, the focus upon educational purposes becomes less important and quality schooling erodes. The evidence is clear: when the principal and faculty communicate and enact a compelling vision of schooling that coincides with parental interests, students benefit from the school's program (Bryk, Lee, & Holland, 1993; Coleman, Hoffer, & Kilgore, 1982; Coleman & Hoffer, 1987).

The threat posed by the loss of the religious sisters and brothers and priests who staffed Catholic schools during previous generations is something that can be dealt with. To meet the challenge, those charged with educational leadership within the U.S. Catholic community must provide formative training for aspiring and practicing Catholic school principals. They must be prepared to communicate the nature and purpose of Catholic schooling and to lead others to reflect upon the fundamental purposes that give life to and guide this important apostolate.

• The evolution of the NCEA's *Catholic Educational Leadership* Monograph Series...

The NCEA's *Catholic Educational Leadership* monograph series has evolved from an extended national conversation concerning this issue. Not only are the number of religious sisters and brothers and priests in school declining, the number of religious vocations is also declining. But, rather than bemoan this trend, the Catholic community must look forward and prepare for a future that will be characterized by increased lay responsibility for many of the Church's temporal activities. Without doubt, if Catholic schools are to survive, the laity will have to respond to God's call and bear the responsibility for providing for the moral and intellectual formation of youth. In order to fulfill their call and its concomitant responsibilities, these men and women will need a specialized formation in order to build upon the legacy bequeathed by their forebears.

Nationally, there have been many efforts to provide this type of formative training. The United States Catholic Conference has published a three-volume preparation program for future and neophyte principals, *Formation and Development for Catholic School Leaders*. Villanova University has sponsored the national satellite teleconference series, *Renewing the Heritage*, which brought together aspiring and practicing Catholic educational leaders with recognized experts from Catholic higher education. Several Catholic colleges and universities boast programs specially designed to train Catholic educational leaders. For example, the University of San Francisco's Institute for Catholic Educational Leadership exemplifies how Catholic higher education can work to provide aspiring Catholic educational leaders the formation they need to lead the nation's Catholic schools. At the University of Notre Dame, the Alliance for Catholic Education prepares young Catholic adults to teach in dioceses experiencing a shortage of qualified Catholic educators. Maybe, in the long run, the Alliance will provide a new stream of vocations to the Catholic educational apostolate and perhaps some Alliance graduates will become the next generation's Catholic educational leaders. Lastly, several of the nation's Catholic institutions of higher education have collaborated to publish *Catholic Education: A Journal of Inquiry and Practice*. After two decades of silence, there once again exists a venue for thoughtful and extended scholarly as well as practical conversation about the issues and problems challenging U.S. Catholic education.

Yet, despite these advances, the challenge of forming those whom God calls to serve as Catholic educational leaders remains. These disciples deserve as much formative training as is possible without duplicating already existing institutional efforts and depleting scarce resources further.

• Who these monographs are intended for...

The NCEA's *Catholic Educational Leadership* monograph series is designed to supplement and extend currently existing efforts by providing access to literature integrating Catholic educational philosophy, theology, and history with the best available educational leadership theory and practice. Intended primarily for aspiring and practicing principals, the monograph series is also directed at other Catholic educational leaders: graduate students in Catholic educational leadership programs; superintendents; pastors and seminarians; and, Catholic educators, parents, as well as members of Catholic school boards.

For principals, each volume provides insight into the nature of educational purposing, albeit from a distinctively Catholic perspective. The variety of topics in the series presents a wide breadth of ideas and practices conveying how principals might lead their schools to preserve and perfect their Catholic identity.

For graduate students in Catholic educational leadership programs and aspiring principals in diocesan-sponsored training programs, each volume provides a compendium of philosophical, theological, and historical research describing the nature of educational leadership from a distinctively Catholic perspective. The bibliography identifies where graduate students and participants in diocesan-sponsored training programs may find primary sources in order that they may put this valuable literature to practical use.

If the Catholic community is to provide formative training for educators in its schools, it is most likely that success will hinge largely upon the efforts of diocesan superintendents. As the chief educational officer of the diocese, each superintendent bears responsibility not only for the professional development of teachers and administrators staffing diocesan schools. The superintendent also bears responsibility for their formative development as Catholic educators. Diocesan superintendents will find in the *Catholic Educational Leadership* monograph series an expansive array of ideas and topics that will not only challenge them to reflect upon how they exercise their leadership role but also how they might exercise that role by providing formative training for educators in diocesan schools.

Many pastors, particularly those who were ordained after the close of the Second Vatican Council, have not been exposed to Catholic educational thought and may feel uncomfortable, if not reluctant, to approach their congregations about educational issues. It must be asked: What could be of more importance to a pastor than the future of his congregation, that is, the children and young men and women who will grow into Catholic adulthood in the opening decades of the new millennium? In each volume, pastors and seminarians will discover provocative ideas intended to foster reflection upon how they might fulfill their pastoral responsibility to preach to their congregations about significant educational matters, whether or not the parish sponsors a Catholic school.

Finally, the NCEA's *Catholic Educational Leadership* monograph series endeavors to provide Catholic educators, parents, and members of Catholic school boards topical guides to stimulate reflection upon and discussion about the important educational responsibilities they bear. After having studied the materials contained in each volume, it is hoped that these individuals will be enabled to make better informed decisions about what they ought to do on behalf of the boys and girls and young men and women whom God has entrusted to their care. All too often, these important parental, Church, and civic responsibilities are relegated to public officials and nameless and faceless bureaucrats who have little or no acquaintance with or interest in enacting Catholic educational thought for the benefit of youth.

• Inter-Institutional collaboration on behalf of Catholic Education...

Through the collaborative efforts of the Department of Education and Human Services at Villanova University and the NCEA's Chief Administrators of Catholic Education Department (CACE), outstanding Catholic educational theorists are joining together in a long range project to provide aspiring and practicing Catholic educational leaders literature to support their ministerial formation.

As series editor, Fr. Richard Jacobs, O.S.A., of Villanova University, is recruiting outstanding Catholic educators to develop reflective guides that will enable Catholic educational leaders to learn and to think about their important role in fostering school improvement, with a particular focus on their school's Catholic identity. His experience, both as a teacher and administrator in Catholic middle and secondary schools as well as his work in Catholic higher education and as a consultant to

Catholic dioceses and schools nationwide, has provided Fr. Jacobs the background to understand the formative needs of Catholic educational leaders and to translate those needs into successful programs. In addition, his editorial experience enables Fr. Jacobs to shepherd texts from inception through publication.

Daniel F. Curtin, CACE Executive Director, is responsible for series supervision. In this role, Mr. Curtin works with Fr. Jacobs to oversee the development of each volume, ensuring that these publications are not only theoretically beneficial but also of practical significance for aspiring and practicing Catholic educational leaders. As an experienced expert in Catholic education, Mr. Curtin possesses the local and national perspective to oversee the development of a monograph series that will not duplicate but will enhance the projects and programs already functioning to form a new generation of Catholic educational leaders.

This inter-institutional collaborative effort on behalf of Catholic education is an important step forward. Bringing together representatives from Catholic higher education, a national Catholic educational organization, and seasoned Catholic educational leaders to develop a monograph series for aspiring and practicing Catholic educational leaders portends a good future. By sharing their diverse gifts on behalf of Catholic education, the Body of Christ will be enriched as Catholic educational thought is renewed through the formation of the next generation of Catholic educational leaders.

• Using the monographs...

Each volume published in the NCEA's *Catholic Educational Leadership* monograph series is not solely a scholarly reflection about the nature and purpose of Catholic educational leadership. While each volume does include some scholarly reflection, the content also provides aspiring and practicing Catholic school principals practical guidance about how they might think about their vocation to lead the community of the Catholic school as well as how they might engage in Catholic educational purposing.

Each volume, then, is written in a style that includes practical applications and is formatted to provide reflective questions and activities along the expanded outside margins. These questions and activities help readers to focus—in very practical ways—upon ideas and concepts deemed essential to Catholic educational leadership. Readers are urged to take notes and to write down their thoughts and ideas as they read each volume so that, as readers think about and plan to exercise Catholic educational leadership in the schools entrusted to their ministry, they can return to their jottings and apply them to the situations confronting them in actual practice.

Were readers to complete and reflect upon the questions and

activities included in the margins as well as to engage in the practical activities spurred by each volume of the NCEA's *Catholic Educational Leadership* monograph series, readers would find themselves better prepared to engage in Catholic educational purposing. Not only would readers possess a more comprehensive understanding about the nature of Catholic educational leadership; in addition, they would also have developed action plans for translating the philosophical, theological, and historical ideals of the Catholic educational heritage into actual practice in their schools. The content of each volume, then, is not a dogmatic pronouncement mandating what Catholic educational leaders must to do in their ministry, as if the NCEA's *Catholic Educational Leadership* monograph series provides a "how to" cookbook of educational leadership recipes for principals to duplicate in Catholic schools. Rather, the philosophical, theological, and historical concepts included in each volume are intended to encourage a reflective practice perspective (Argyris & Schön, 1974; Beyer, 1991; Brubacher, Case, & Reagan, 1994; Dewey, 1910; Schön, 1991; Sergiovanni, 1986, 1995a) that focuses directly upon what Catholic educational leadership involves and the principles upon which Catholic educational leadership might be exercised in the nation's Catholic schools.

While the decline of religious sisters and brothers and priests in schools can be viewed as a threat to the future of Catholic education, the interest expressed by many lay men and women to follow in the footsteps of their forebears presents a tremendous resource and opportunity for the Catholic community. As the identity of the Catholic school is equated more with educational purposing than the fact of whether or not school's principal and teachers are religious sisters and brothers or priests, Catholic educational leaders can take advantage of the opportunity to form the new generation of lay Catholic educational leaders. Alongside Christ, who is the Teacher, these devoted men and women will carry forward the purpose of Catholic education into the 21st century, just as their religious forebears did at the turn of the 20th century.

On the Solemnity of
Mary the Mother of God
January 1, 2001

Richard Jacobs, O.S.A.
Villanova University

Daniel F. Curtin
National Catholic
Educational Association

Editor's Preface

Unless the Lord build the house,
they labor in vain who build it.
(Psalm 127:1)

The Psalmist's words provide a most fitting and appropriate theological focus for this fourth volume in the NCEA's *Catholic Educational Leadership* Monograph Series. "Unless the Lord build the house"—that is, unless the source and animating core of Catholic schooling is the inspiring mission drawn from Scripture and Church tradition and unless this is made palpable and vibrant in each and every Catholic school—"they labor in vain who build it." These blunt words resound like a clarion to remind Catholic educational leaders that absent the Lord—who is *the* Builder—their efforts to build effective Catholic schools are for naught.

• Catholic educational leadership practice: integrating science and theology...

At the outset and by means of introduction to this volume, it should be noted that many educational theorists and practitioners vehemently disagree with the Psalmist's assertion. Operating out of an ideology that attributes school effectiveness not to any subjective theological category but to objective scientific categories, these researchers and practitioners have directed much of their attention to what women and men in schools do to foster effectiveness (Blumberg & Greenfield, 1980; Brookover & Lezotte, 1979; *Effective Instructional Management*, 1983; Ellett, 1992; Fullan, 1993, 1997; Hughes, 1999; Lambert, 1998; Murphy, 1990; Teddlie, 1994; Zappulla, 1983). Not surprisingly, these individuals direct their primary focus upon those characteristics attributed to educational leaders whose activities are purported to "cause" effective schools.

For their part, researchers have formulated a "knowledge base" which explicates these "best practices." Furthermore, these researchers have proposed that these should be inculcated in aspiring educational leaders (Boyan, 1998; Culbertson, 1988; Griffiths, 1988; Murphy & Louis, 1999; Smith & Piele, 1989; Thomson, 1992, 1993).

To no one's surprise, then, practitioners training to be educational leaders are exposed to this knowledge base, the idea being that, as educational leaders, these individuals will use these tools as the primary conceptual lens for thinking about and evaluating what they should do in actual practice. Graduates report, however, that teaching and learning in educational administration programs is largely irrelevant to the complexities they confront in practice (Fowler, 1991; Goldman & Kempner, 1988; Hemphill, Griffiths, & Fredriksen, 1962; Schnur, 1989). A few dissent from this opinion—not surprisingly—those who earn doctorates in educational administration (Wildman, 1991).

What is important, however, is not the disjoint between theory and practice but what unites the researchers and practitioners. Both are bound by an ideology, specifically, that science can specify that which constitutes best practice and this knowledge base ultimately will perfect schools and render them more effective.

The purpose of *Architects of Catholic Culture* is not to debunk this ideology nor its implications for practice. After all, Catholic schools are schools first and science can function as a trustworthy and erstwhile ally in the effort to make Catholic schools more effective. As the author of this volume, Professor Timothy Cook (Creighton University), rightly notes, "Catholic" is an adjective modifying the noun "school." Consonant with the Congregation for Catholic Education (1988), Cook maintains that Catholic schools are first and foremost schools and must be effective schools. Because of this fact, then, research is helpful because it identifies and provides instructive guidance about what educational leaders can do to foster effectiveness in their schools. It is incumbent upon Catholic educational leaders—because Catholic schools are schools first—to utilize this knowledge base when envisioning and setting an agenda for making Catholic schools more effective.

At the same time, however, the Psalmist's words remind Catholic educational leaders that unless the Lord builds the school, as *Catholic*, they labor in vain who build it.

Alert to this theological focus, Cook asserts that Catholic educational leadership requires something more than utilizing the tools and skills associated with best practice inculcated in educational leadership training programs, a perspective that likens Catholic educational leadership to a job where one simply implements tools and skills in practice episodes. That "something more"—the value added-dimension of Catholic educational leadership—is a comprehensive plan conceived and designed by Catholic educational leaders which intentionally builds Catholic culture in schools. These dedicated women and men elevate and transform what would otherwise be a secular job into a religious vocation and build what would otherwise be a secular institution into a faith community.

• Catholic educational leadership practice: focusing on school culture...

During the late-1980s and 1990s, some educational researchers moved away from the predominant scientific ideology guiding educational theory as they directed their focus upon the concept of school culture. Building on Schein's (1992) pioneering efforts to identify organizational culture and, furthermore, to demonstrate how leaders "build" culture in a variety of organizations, these educational researchers applied this concept to schools. The consensus of opinion is that school culture is a crucial factor in school effectiveness (Brookover, Beady, Flood,

Schweitzer & Wisenbaker, 1979; Brookover & Lezotte, 1979; Grant, 1981, 1982, 1985; Lightfoot, 1983; Purkey & Smith, 1982, 1983; Rutter, Maughan, Mortimore, Ouston, & Smith 1979). In addition, others have maintained that attentiveness to building culture characterizes principals in effective schools (Corbett, Firestone, & Rossman, 1987; Deal, 1985, 1993; Deal & Peterson, 1990, 1999; Fullan, 1993, 1997).

In light of this expanding body of research, one of the crucial challenges confronting educational leaders in all school settings involves creating, maintaining, and perfecting the school's culture so that everything in the school supports its educative mission. And yet, as crucial as the challenge of building culture in schools may well be, the idea of school culture and the principal's leadership role in building it has only recently received scant attention.

Perhaps much of this lack of attention is, for the most part, attributable to American culture itself. That is, for much of the 20th century, many well-intentioned citizens have subscribed implicitly to the notion that schools exist to provide the nation's youth the intellectual and moral formation they need if they are to accept the mantle of civic responsibility in the next generation. But, the way this notion has been translated into actual practice in schools has been premised upon the assumption that schools are *institutions*. As institutions, schools employ teachers who provide youth instruction in the curricular areas that bring the school's institutional purpose to fruition.

Although there appears to be little in this assumption to disagree with, hindsight provides a trustworthy guide for a reconsideration. Indeed, the argument can be sustained that the institutionalization of schooling has rendered impersonal much of what transpires in schools, that is, if they are to fulfill their educative mission. As Cusick (1992) incisively argues, schooling in the United States has developed into a monolith, a system having its own nature and logic, evidencing a culture that steers the human beings who constitute this system along a defined route. For example, teachers fill the institutional role of providing instruction. Students are in schools to learn curricular content. And, the principal's role is to ensure that instruction and learning transpire in the most efficient and effective way. Because this logic is a grammar that frames how people look at schooling (Tyack & Tobin, 1994), thinking about schools as institutions makes eminent sense and goes uncontested.

Lest it be forgotten, organizations are a consequence of the patterns of communication and action between human beings (Simon, 1945/1997). In light of this, the emphasis upon the institutional dimension of schools renders human beings into nameless, faceless functionaries, persons who fill roles, are easily replaced by others (as certainly they all will be), and who ultimately bear no personal responsibility for their words and actions (Jackall, 1988; Wolgast, 1992). In addition, this institutional emphasis reduces the acquisition of instructional content to factual matters that must be assessed objectively, that is, as these factual matters are measured on state-mandated standardized tests. And, success in providing instruction evidences itself as a school's aggregate scores on standardized tests demonstrate superiority when compared to institutional peers and competitors. Yes, institutions can be tidy and orderly...yet utterly devoid of anything distinctively human.

In institutions like these, students, teachers, and principals move along trajectories in much the same way that airplanes, boats, and trains follow pre-planned trajectories. In flight, airplanes pass by one another but, for safety's sake, never too closely. In the sea, boats accord one another a wide berth and issue signals to ensure that they never come too close. And, although trains pass swiftly by one another, they do so because the tracks they follow never converge. Likewise, students, teachers, and principals bypass one another frequently in these institutions as they go about their business. But, they never run into, meet, or interact with one another. In short, there is no human organization (Simon, 1945/1997)—only an impersonal institution—with the sad consequence that school "isn't fun anymore" (Lightfoot, 1983).

To counteract this impersonalism and the deleterious effects it has upon the human beings whose lives intersect in schools, a minority of some more philosophically oriented educational researchers have devoted attention to conceiving of schools as *communities* and what this metaphorical change implies for people in schools. For his part, Sergiovanni (1994a, 1995b) has steadfastly maintained that by changing the metaphor used to describe schools, it is possible to change the reality itself because the new metaphor offers a way for people to reconceptualize the school and its educative mission. For example, in a school community, students couldn't simply pass through each teacher's classroom. Likewise, teachers couldn't simply look upon their work as providing instruction. And, principals couldn't simply make pronouncements, issue memos, or dictate what is in the school's best interests. No, in a school community, students, teachers, and principals must meet one another and interact with one another as human beings, not as interchangeable functionaries in the monolith of an impersonal, institutional, bureaucratic machine.

The challenge for any educational leader, then, is to build a distinctive culture in the community of the school. Cook reminds Catholic educational leaders, however, that Catholic school culture is "a 'way of life,' rooted in Christ, a Gospel-based creed and code, and a Catholic vision that provides inspiration and identity, is shaped over time, and is passed from one generation to the next through devices that capture and stimulate the Catholic imagination..." (p. 16).

• Catholic educational leadership practice: building Catholic culture in diverse contexts...

One of the most significant—albeit hotly debated—research findings is that Catholic schools appear to be effective because of the "social capital" drawn from the strong culture that is supportive of both the school and its religious mission (Coleman, 1982; Coleman *et al.*, 1987). Validating the research of the minority of theorists who argue that schools are communities, it is the communal dimension that characterizes Catholic schooling. Evidently, this culture exerts a statistically significant influence upon the people in Catholic schools as well as upon the educational outcomes associated with Catholic schools, especially urban Catholic schools serving minority populations (Bryk *et al.*, 1993; Coleman *et al.*, 1982; Coleman & Hoffer, 1987).

As Cook reminds his readers, the communal dimension of Catholic schooling is built upon women and men who possess a profound respect for human beings, each of whom is created in God's image and likeness. These teachers and principals are not artificial persons filling institutional roles (Wolgast, 1992). No, they are authentic human beings who have real names and faces, who bear responsibility for their decisions and, because of their unique humanity, are not able to be replaced as persons even though they all will be replaced in their functional roles. Of such people, Maritain noted more than five decades ago, "...to advance in this self-perfection is not to copy an ideal. It is to let yourself be led by another where you did not want to go, and to let Divine Love Who calls each being by his own name mold you and make you a person, a true original, not a copy" (1943, p. 36). Years after their service on behalf of youth, their students spin sagas and myths about these disciples—the genuine heroines and heroes of Catholic school culture.

The communal dimension of Catholic schools gives appropriate emphasis to the notion that learning isn't simply the acquisition of instructional content. Indeed, learning also requires that youth become a particular kind of person and, in Catholic schools, a character imbued with Gospel values. To achieve these intellectual and moral outcomes—the Catholic school's cultural purpose—Cook asserts that Catholic school culture must evidence strong interpersonal relationships forged within a community of faith. Yes, in Catholic schools, factual matters can be and must be assessed, perhaps on standardized tests. But, success in this communal endeavor is not solely a matter of the scores students achieve but is, more so, a matter of human beings who *through their personal interactions* translate Gospel values into words, actions, and experiences that give fuller expression to what Catholic school culture values. Daily life in these school communities may be somewhat messy and turbulent...but never devoid of humanity.

Architects of Catholic Culture brings into proper relief the limits of the scientific ideology associated with much of the theorizing about the institution of 20th-century American schooling. This monograph offers Catholic educational leaders a way to conceptualize Catholic schooling and to reflect upon their crucial role—a professional role but also, and more importantly, a ministerial role—in building effective Catholic school communities. In previous eras of U.S. Catholic educational history, the word "permeation" suggested a similar, though more restricted notion, linking Catholic school culture with secular subjects like math and science and the absolute value placed upon importance of conjoining the school's Catholic identity with every subject in the curriculum. In this volume, Cook expands the idea of permeation to include something deeper, more elusive, and more enduring across the generations: the school's Catholic culture. For Catholic educational leaders at least one implication of Cook's notion is clear: to the extent to which they work alongside Christ in building Catholic school culture—a faith community imbued by Gospel values—Catholic educators will exert a profound personal influence upon the true subject of Catholic education, that is, the student (Jacobs, 1997, pp. 52-62).

To assist these dedicated women and men in their ministry, this newest addition to the NCEA's *Catholic Educational Leadership* monograph series provides building plans to spur Catholic educational leaders to contemplate how they might collaborate with the Lord in transforming the routine managerial aspects of the principalship into a ministry on behalf of and for the Church. These women and men are not artificial persons—nameless and faceless functionaries filling institutional roles for a period of time—but disciples, the architects of Catholic culture. Together with the Lord, these disciples do not labor in vain. Instead, they endeavor to design and build Catholic school cultures that intentionally provide youth the intellectual and moral formation they deserve so that they will capably lead the next generation as adult Catholic citizens.

Introduction

Were someone to place a frog in a pan of cold water and light a Bunsen burner beneath the pan, as the heat is gradually increased, the frog will not jump from the pan but will instead remain in it...until the frog boils to death. The explanation given for this "boiled frog" phenomenon is that the environment changes so slowly that it triggers no immediate response. Thus, when the frog finally senses what is happening, it is too late to respond.

Tichy and Devanna (1986) used this analogy in the 1980s to illustrate what would happen to American corporations if they did not respond to the rapid pace of global change. Likewise, during the 1970s, rising tuition, presumed mediocre academics, and a shrinking pool of students sounded a similar alarm for the nation's Catholic schools. To avoid the boiled frog phenomenon, Catholic educators had to raise academic standards or risk having their schools relegated to a footnote in educational history.

Like the most successful American corporations, Herculean efforts to improve the nation's Catholic schools have proven successful as they now are highly regarded by researchers and the general public alike. Never in U.S. Catholic educational history have Catholic schools received such recognition.

the decline of religious sisters and brothers and priests...

While it is true that Catholic schools are schools first, their religious mission provides their guiding purpose. Prior to Vatican II, preserving Catholic identity was less of an issue because religious sisters and brothers and priests staffed the schools almost exclusively (Jacobs, 1998a,b,c). In that era, as these dedicated women and men tackled many pressing academic and financial crises, Catholic identity was not a focal issue. During the past 30 years, however, the number of religious and priests serving in the nation's Catholic schools has declined precipitously. In the past decade, the percentage has been halved, declining from 16% to under 7% (McDonald, 2000, p. 19). Now that the laity staff Catholic schools almost entirely, by default they must assume responsibility for the Catholic identity of these schools.

a personal experience and response...

Neophyte Catholic school principals experience defining moments after assuming the mantle of religious leadership. As a lay principal, my defining moment occurred when I got up to lead the student assembly in prayer for the first time. Calm on the outside but trembling on the inside, I vividly remember seeing some students snicker as I made the Sign of the Cross. At that moment two realizations struck me. First, even though I knew one of the reasons I was hired was to re-establish the school's Catholic identity, it was only when I was standing on the stage and saw some students snickering that I grasped what an uphill battle it would be. Secondly, even though I was fresh from a graduate program in Catholic educational leadership and even though I am a religious person, I felt ill-prepared to serve as a religious leader.

Over the years, I grew frustrated as I struggled to be a religious leader and to re-establish the school's Catholic identity, especially because virtually all of the writing and speeches concerning Catholic identity was very theoretical. It seemed that most treatments began and ended with the thesis: "Catholic identity is a critical issue that needs to be addressed." Yet, the rhetoric never quite reached the next level—where Catholic identity is defined and illustrated in concrete terms that can be considered and then applied in diverse settings. Catholic identity has remained, for the most part, an elusive concept stuck somewhere "out there."

two metaphors shaping thought and behavior...

In *Metaphors We Live By,* Lakoff and Johnson (1980) suggest that "the essence of metaphor is understanding and experiencing one kind of thing in terms of another" (p. 5). Using metaphors to study organizations, Bolman and Deal (1997) suggest that, in as far as organizations are concerned, metaphors can "make the strange familiar and the familiar strange" (p. 229).

Architects of Catholic Culture uses metaphors to make theoretical and abstract concepts more concrete. Two metaphors provide the conceptual framework for this volume: "culture" and "architecture." The metaphor of culture, especially as it applies to Catholic schools, serves as the central concept because culture conjures up full-bodied and robust concepts like core beliefs and values, heroes and heroines, symbols, ritual traditions, human communication, history, as well as those characters whose behavior and antics influence and shape culture. Culture also influences what women and men value, why they act the way they do, and how they interact with others. The second metaphor, architecture, provides a medium to examine culture especially with regard to "building" culture in a Catholic school. This volume's unifying theme—that Catholic educational leaders are architects of Catholic culture—marries these two metaphors to inform Catholic educational leadership practice.

Catholic educational leaders as God's architects...

Scripture frequently uses the metaphor of architecture. One notable example is Peter's assertion to the Sanhedrin with reference to Jesus: "He is 'the stone rejected by you, the builders, which has become the cornerstone' " (Acts 4: 11). In addition, the image of "building" depicts how Jesus' disciples would usher in the Kingdom of God. Is it only incidental that the Gospels portray Jesus as a carpenter?

The metaphor of architecture helps to clarify how one might enhance Catholic culture because architecture connotes artistry and cultural expression in addition to form and function. Consider, for example, that not all buildings are architectural wonders. Is a tool shed the equivalent of a skyscraper? Is a hovel the equivalent of a cathedral? Obviously not. Architecture expresses what humans value and communicates attributes like power, strength, extravagance, simplicity, convenience, or innovation. Certainly, what church buildings express is different from what theaters and government buildings express. Does not a Catholic school by virtue of its religious identity embody an added dimension? Should not a Catholic school communicate what it upholds as sacred through its cultural architecture?

The metaphor of architecture provides another useful point of comparison in the person of the architect who is the designer, the key player in a building project from its inception to its completion. The architect formulates the idea, designs the plan, and oversees construction. In the design stage, the architect considers building materials and determines appropriate methods of construction. The architect completes all of this planning mindful of the particular building site and its surrounding environment. Indeed, an architect would be foolhardy to design a building without considering climate and terrain, among other factors.

As a leader in the early Christian church, St. Paul refers to himself as a builder. "According to the grace of God given to me, like a wise master builder I lay the foundations of faith, and others build on what I have laid" (1 Corinthians 3:10). As a builder of God's kingdom, the religious leader is a visionary who designs the plans for preserving, enhancing, and communicating what is sacred. Furthermore, the leader oversees the building of this culture, taking into account cultural environment, available and desirable materials, and one's leadership style. Like an architect, then, the Catholic educational leader is the "master builder" of Catholic school culture.

the title of this monograph ...

The title *"Architects of Catholic Culture"* is derived from "God's bricklayers," the nickname Dennis Cardinal Dougherty of Philadelphia used jokingly to refer to himself (Connelly, 1976, p. 380). It is the metaphor Jacobs borrowed to characterize the nation's Catholic religious leaders in the early- to mid-20th century who initiated and oversaw the building of scores of schools, hospitals, and other Catholic institutions (1998b, p. 15).

Like those religious leaders of the early- to mid-1900s, today's Catholic educational leaders are also engaged in a building program. Yet, unlike their forebears whose goal it was to consecrate cornerstones and expand Catholic influence throughout the nation, the goal for today's

Catholic educational leaders is more similar to St. Paul's—to design and build Catholic culture. Therefore, by reiterating the metaphor, "God's bricklayers," and substituting the term "architect" for St. Paul's self-reference as "master builder," today's Catholic educational leaders serve as this generation's "architects of Catholic culture."

an overview of this monograph...

Architects of Catholic Culture consists of 10 chapters. Chapter 1 considers the concept of culture from its definition to its theoretical background and practical application in a variety of settings. Chapter 2 focuses on organizational culture as it applies to Catholic schools. This chapter offers a definition of Catholic school culture and conceptualizes what is distinctive about a Catholic school's "way of life." Chapters 3–9 describe seven different "building blocks" of cultural architecture— core beliefs and values, heroes and heroines, symbols, ritual tradition, human communication, history, and cultural players. The first part of each chapter applies the "building blocks" introduced in Chapter 1 to Catholic schools. The second part of each chapter offers a "building plan" that Catholic educational leaders might consider applying in their setting. Chapter 10 is the keystone binding together all that precedes. Chapter 10 provides more than a summary, however. It offers conclusions, principles, and propositions that challenge Catholic educational leaders to consider in their role as architects of Catholic culture.

the purpose of this monograph...

Architects of Catholic Culture challenges practicing and aspiring Catholic educational leaders to consider the substantive matters that subsume Catholic identity, that is, the culture of a Catholic school and the leader's role in preserving and enhancing that culture. Implicit is the assumption that Catholic culture does not happen by itself nor does it occur through osmosis. Metaphorically speaking, the educational leader functions as the architect of Catholic culture.

The purpose of *Architects of Catholic Culture*, then, is to stimulate further reflection about the concept of Catholic identity and the building of Catholic culture so that the laity who serve as Catholic educational leaders will better understand the cultural dimension of their leadership responsibility. And, as a result of developing a sound building plan, these women and men will experience the satisfaction that, like their forebears in previous generations, they too have been effective in their role as architects of Catholic culture.

Chapter 1

• Organizational culture and its origins...

In an effort to examine groups of people, especially in relation to one another, anthropologists have forged an area of scholarly endeavor, that of "cultural studies." Early research sought to explain why, for example, some cultures are warlike while others are more peaceful, why some cultures trade while others hunt, and why some cultures are stable and long-lasting while others are transitory. Later research examined values and their interaction in a variety of cultures.

By the mid-1900s theorists applied many of these principles to the study of organizations. Early research (Arnold, 1938; Barnard, 1938; Selznik, 1957) provided useful insights into organizational behavior, for example, but failed to generate widespread enthusiasm. Although others preceded him, Schein (1992) is considered the pioneer in the study of organizational culture due to his development of a conceptual framework for this area of research.

definitions of organizational culture...

The adjectives "slippery" and "intangible" describe the nature of organizational culture. Regardless of how scholars define "culture" (Figure 1, p. 6), the definitions identify to some common themes. For example, organizational culture points to a group's "soul," giving meaning to a group's existence and experience. Organizational culture also helps define individuals, providing a framework for thinking and feeling, a code for relationships, and a lens for interpreting events and the world. Organizational culture appears to be the "glue" that provides continuity and stability and binds a people together. In essence, organizational culture is a "way of life" within a particular organization.

corporate culture

In the early 1980s, scholars popularized these theories and concepts for the corporate world. Peters and Waterman (1982) believe the trend began on October 27, 1980, when *Business Week* ran the cover story "Corporate culture: The hard-to-change values that spell success or failure." Soon, a string of bestsellers touted the importance of managing corporate culture. In 1982, Peters and Waterman's *In Search of Excellence* and Deal and Kennedy's *Corporate Cultures: The Rites and Rituals of Corporate Life* asserted that strong corporate culture contributes to productivity and success.

Scholars generally agree that a unique culture characterizes corporations and that corporate leaders must attend to this dimension of organizational life to ensure peak performance. To fully identify and understand a corporation's "deep" culture, leaders must look beyond these more tangible expressions to the intangible values embedded within. It is here, lurking beneath the surface, where corporate leaders discover what others hold sacred. Astute leaders know that it is at this level that issues must be addressed if long-lasting change in performance and productivity is to take place.

Figure 1.
Definitions of organizational culture

Culture is...
- The way we do things around here. (Bower, 1966, p. 22)
- The system of values, symbols, and shared meanings of a group including the embodiment of these values, symbols, and meanings into material objects and ritualized practices. Culture governs what is of worth for a particular group and how group members should think, feel, and behave. (Sergiovanni & Corbally, 1984, p. viii)
- A historically rooted, socially transmitted set of deep patterns of thinking and ways of acting that give meaning to human experience, that unconsciously dictate how experience is seen, assessed, and acted on. (Deal & Peterson, 1990, p. 8)
- A pattern of shared basic assumptions that the group learned as it solved its problems of external adaptation and internal integration, that has worked well enough to be considered valid and, therefore, to be taught to new members as the correct way to perceive, think, and feel in relation to those problems. (Schein, 1992, p. 12)

Catholic culture

Segueing from the boardroom to the pulpit is more natural than one might think. Deal and Kennedy (1982) offer the Roman Catholic Church as one of the best management models for the future because of its strong, enduring culture and cohesion despite its atomized parish structure. Besides the truths that the Church professes and the values it represents, people are attracted to the Church, the authors assert, because of its "soul, spirit, magic, heart, ethos, mission, saga" (p. 195). They conclude that the yearning for these ideals is fundamental to human experience and that the corporations which will be most successful in the future will be those that have addressed these fundamental needs.

According to Greeley (1990, p. 44), human beings search for meaning in their lives. For most people, religion provides that meaning. Reduced to a common denominator, religion provides a purpose, a code of behavior, and a lens for interpreting the world. The European experience supports Greeley's contention that religion is not just a subset of culture but rather something absorbed by culture to the point that religion becomes virtually indistinguishable from the rest of culture.

Lynch broadens this view of faith, expanding it beyond creed and code to life experience and culture, positing that "imagination" is necessary to interpret the world through the eyes of faith (cited in Bednar, 1996, p. 152). For Lynch, humans use images to order and understand reality. Humans also use metaphors to make the strange familiar and to anchor new knowledge in previous knowledge. Because the ways humans imagine reality color their interpretation of the world, faith is more than a function of the intellect or the activity of belief; rather, it is a way of experiencing life. Thought and image are mutually supportive and imagination, as Lynch describes it, is not fantasy but a source of revelation. For example, the arts, as cultural expressions, serve to arouse faith (p. 138). Based on this theory, Catholic educational leaders—as architects of Catholic culture—should ensure that their schools have strong fine arts programs.

The concept of faith as imagination has evolved into the notion of "Catholic imagination" as a synonym or antecedent for Catholic culture. Popularized by Greeley in such works as *The Catholic Myth* (1990) and *The Catholic Imagination* (2000), the concept of Catholic imagination begs the question: "Do Catholics experience religion differently from Protestants?" Theologians including Groome (1996, 1998), Hellwig (1995), McBrien (1994), and Tracy (1981) concur that Catholics possess a sacramental view of society, the world, and human experience. That is to say, Catholics believe in the fundamental goodness of society and see the world as a place where God is actively present and revealed. Standing in stark contrast is the Protestant view that society and the world are devoid of God, save rare events like the death and resurrection of Jesus. The Catholic experience of life's "sacramentality," reflected in the Church's seven sacraments, punctuates life's passages, in contrast to the Protestant emphasis on the sacraments of Baptism and Holy Communion.

Greeley (1995) contends that even though many U.S. Catholics disagree with Church teaching on such issues as contraception and women's ordination, they stay in the Church because Catholicism appeals to their religious imagination. "…[T]hey do in fact stay because of the attractiveness of Catholic metaphors" (p. 31). To Greeley and others, Catholic identity and culture are perhaps more a function of a distinctive imagination of faith than they are a function of dogma.

The natural tension between unity and diversity presents an interesting paradox for the U.S. Catholic Church in reference to identity, culture, and imagination. To be a cohesive Church culture, must everyone imagine the same? Fitzpatrick (1987) argues that one challenge confronting the U.S. Catholic Church is to broaden its understanding of Catholic imagination in order to accommodate an increasingly diverse congregation.

Reflect upon your "Catholic imagination" and that present in your school:

- *What Catholic rituals, images, or metaphors have enhanced your experience of God?*
- *Do you have memories of your experiences in a Catholic school, especially as a student, that have heightened your Catholic imagination?*
- *Do any occasions come to mind when, as a principal, you have heightened the Catholic imagination of your students?*
- *Is there a diversity of cultures and faith traditions present in your school community? How do you accommodate them?*

Identify what you might do to heighten Catholic imagination in your school and to be more inclusive of diverse cultural and faith traditions:

1. _____
   _____
2. _____
   _____
3. _____
   _____

There is another irony concerning the intersection of Catholicism and culture that is worth noting. In *The Churching of America, 1776-1990*, Finke and Stark (1992) hypothesize that the denominations which are the most countercultural, demanding of their members, and distinctive in nature, experience the highest rate of growth. Adds Finke: "High fertility rates, immigration, and aggressive marketing all fuel this growth, but the religion's intense faith and distinctive subculture retain the faithful" (p. 34). People tend to value religion on the basis of how costly it is to belong—the more one must sacrifice in order to be in good standing, the more valuable the religion....the more 'mainline' the church (in the sense of being regarded as 'respectable' and 'reasonable'), the lower the value of belonging to it, and this eventually results in widespread defection" (p. 238).

What implications does the notion of Catholic imagination present to Catholic educational leaders? Several can be identified. First, in a treatment of Lynch's contribution to the theological understanding of faith as imagination, Bednar (1996) advises pastors—and this could apply to Catholic educational leaders as well—that church leaders should attend to the images of faith as much as they do to the doctrine of faith. "Images are not mere 'attention getters' in homilies. Images speak, think, and feel. They motivate us to act....Even the architecture of the Church building with its use of space, statues, vigil lights, and altar suggest a certain way of speaking, thinking, feeling, and acting. They invite a certain sort of approach to God. They embody the sensibility of faith" (p. 160).

In the school setting, then, it is incumbent upon Catholic educational leaders to capture and attend to the Catholic imagination by utilizing the building blocks of culture including ceremonies, rituals, symbols, and human communication.

Second, as Fitzpatrick (1987) implies, Catholic schools must broaden their interpretation of Catholic imagination to accommodate the diversity of faith traditions that exists in the Church and school populations—Hispanic, African American, Native American, to name a few. To this end, Catholic educational leaders should study and promote the school's heroes and heroines, ritual traditions, symbols, and human communication, among others.

Third, Finke and Stark's (1992) notion challenges Catholic educational leaders to work at ensuring the countercultural dynamic of the faith tradition institutionalized in Catholic schooling. This suggests that Catholic educational leaders must continually ask themselves and other members of the community—especially the students—if the school's culture is any different from that of the local public school. If the culture is not different, perhaps the institutionalization has resulted in aspects of religious culture being taken for granted. Perhaps such a situation should signal the need to examine and correct the ill effects of the institutionalization of faith in an effort to recapture and reinvigorate Catholic religious imagination.

school culture

Deal helped to popularize the concept of school culture (Deal, 1985, 1991, 1993; Deal & Peterson, 1990, 1999), defining school culture as "the character of a school as it reflects deep patterns of values, beliefs, and traditions that have been formed over the course of history" (Deal & Peterson, 1990, p. 7). Culture, then, is the hidden or informal curriculum. It is what graduates remember long after their formal schooling ends.

Visitors can get a sense of a school's culture minutes after walking through its front doors. Much is inferred from the physical layout, decorations on the walls, the way people greet visitors, the school's cleanliness and smell, what students are talking about as they change classes, and how people interact with one another.

Regional accrediting agencies have also acknowledged the value of studying school culture. In fall 1994, the New England Association of Schools and Colleges (NEAS&C) began requiring schools to devote an entire section in their self-study report to school culture. This section concludes the self-study and is considered by NEAS&C to be a "unifying activity" (p. 61).

Study after study assigns primary importance to school culture in determining school effectiveness (Brookover *et al.*, 1979; Brookover & Lezotte, 1979; Grant 1981, 1982, 1985; Lightfoot, 1983; Purkey & Smith, 1983, 1985; Rutter *et al.*, 1979). To drive home the singular importance of culture, Purkey and Smith (1983) declare, "... an effective school is distinguished by its culture..." (p. 68).

Before discussing Catholic school culture, it is important to consider the research citing Catholic schools as models of effectiveness. This research focuses on the "sense of community" that is characteristic of most effective schools (Bryk & Driscoll, 1988; Bryk *et al.*, 1993; Grant, 1981, 1982, 1985; Lightfoot, 1983; Purkey & Smith, 1983, 1985; Rutter, *et al.*, 1979; Sergiovanni, 1994b). Coleman and his colleagues did much to highlight the community dimension of Catholic schools by comparing the effects of public, private, and parochial education using measures such as growth in math and verbal achievement and dropout rates (Coleman *et al.*, 1982; Coleman & Hoffer, 1987). These researchers cite the community feeling of Catholic schools as a prime reason for their success, writing, "The examination of dropouts among students from different backgrounds shows especially striking results. Here the communal character of the Catholic community appears to reduce very sharply the likelihood of dropping out of school" (Coleman & Hoffer, 1987, p. 148).

To explain the underlying strength of the community aspect

"Culture": a shared system of values that influences how members of a group act and feel and interpret the world

Specify three shared values that constitute the soul of your school or your school's "character":

1. _____
2. _____
3. _____

"Climate": an atmosphere dictated by how members view an organization and interact with each other

How are the three values listed above evident in your school's climate:
- *building layout, decorations, smell, and upkeep?*
- *how visitors are greeted?*
- *how members of your school community interact with each other?*
- *what students talk to each other about in between classes?*

Discuss how the culture of your school is different from that of the local public school:

_____

_____

_____

_____

_____

_____

Are there values that you would like to characterize your school's culture?

1. _____

2. _____

3. _____

Identify how you will spearhead the effort to inculturate these values:

1. _____

2. _____

3. _____

of Catholic schools, Coleman *et al.* distinguish between "value" communities and "functional" communities. According to their research, value communities are those in which members share a common set of values. By contrast, functional communities are value communities whose members hold values in common and are closely linked and interact with each other both in and out of the school setting. Coleman and Hoffer (1987) contend that "...the religious community is one of the few remaining strong bases of functional community in modern society which includes both adults and children" (p. 215).

Coleman *et al.* argue that a functional community builds "social capital" in youth. Social capital—the interactive web of relationships of parents with parents, parents with children, and parents with the school—is a resource to draw upon in the formation of youth. Just as financial capital (wealth) and human capital (skills) are assets to be developed, the same holds true for social capital. Coleman and Hoffer (1987) conclude that the results of the research "...emphasize the importance of the embeddedness of young persons in the enclaves of adults most proximate to them, first and most prominently the family and second, a surrounding community of adults (exemplified in all these results by the religious community)" (p. 229).

Effective schools exhibit strong cultures, especially through a strong community spirit. Catholic schools, then, are particularly poised to succeed because of the "social capital" drawn from a strong supporting adult faith community (Coleman *et al.*, 1982; Coleman & Hoffer, 1987). For Catholic educational leaders, at least one implication is clear: to the extent they design and build a functional Catholic school culture—a faith community—this influences academic achievement.

A Catholic educational leader could build a school community without building a faith community. It is incumbent upon Catholic educational leaders, then, to connect their community-building efforts intentionally with the culture of the Catholic Church, given its fullest expression in Scripture and Tradition.

Chapter 2

- **Catholic school culture...**

Since the 1970s, Flynn has studied the effectiveness of Australian Catholic schools in terms of their religious and academic outcomes. In *The Culture of Catholic Schools* (1993), he concludes: "On almost all of the six outcome measures of Catholic schools used in this study— both religious and academic—the *culture of the schools,* as indicated by students' attitudes toward school and their experience of school life, *plays an important role.* Catholic schools do indeed make an important difference!" (p. 393).

Flynn's studies extend secular definitions of organizational culture by defining Catholic school culture this way: "The culture of a Catholic school expresses the core beliefs, values, traditions, symbols and patterns of behaviour which provide meaning to the school community and which help shape the lives of students, teachers, and parents. In short, culture is 'the way we do things around here' " (p. 39).

This research raises an important question: "What is distinctive about Catholic school culture or the way of life in a Catholic school?"

Catholic school identity and educational goals...

At the outset, it must be recalled that before Catholic schools can be anything else, they are schools first. "Catholic" is not the noun in this instance; rather, it is the adjective qualifying the noun. In essence, Catholic schools must be good schools before they can be good Catholic schools. As the National Congress on Catholic Schools for the 21st Century noted: "The commitment to academic excellence, which fosters the intellectual development of faculty and students, is an integral part of the mission of the Catholic school" (1992, p. 17).

Bryk *et al.* (1993) have studied distinctive features of Catholic high schools in relation to school effectiveness. Interestingly, Catholic high school students take a larger core of academic subjects than their counterparts attending similar public high schools. The authors warn that the "shopping mall" culture and low academic standards of some public high schools cause students to "develop unrealistic understandings about work and the adequacy of their current efforts. In contrast to some public high school norms, one rarely succeeds in life by 'just showing up' " (p. 305).

Catholic identity, then, encompasses a religious mission as well as academic excellence centered on the liberal arts. Further broadening this definition, should not the concept of a school's "Catholic identity" include a global/multicultural dimension in recognition of the universality or *catholic* nature of the sponsoring Church? Using the three-pronged definition of Catholic school identity (Figure 2, p. 12), Catholic schools should move into the future as a unique expression of American education.

Grade your school from "A" to "F" in each of these three areas of Catholic school identity:

_____ *Academic Excellence*
_____ *Religious Mission*
_____ *Globalness/ Multiculturalism*

Identify three actions you can take to improve your school's grades:

1. _____
2. _____
3. _____

Figure 2.
Catholic school identity

$$\text{Catholic school identity} = \begin{array}{c} \text{Academic Excellence} \\ + \\ \text{Religious Mission} \\ + \\ \text{Globalness/Multiculturalism} \end{array}$$

Catholic school identity as a "Gospel culture"...

The gravitational pull holding the constellation of Catholic schools together is the concept of an evangelical religious mission. That Catholic schools participate in the Church's mission to "go and teach" (Mt 28: 19-20) cuts to the core of each Catholic school's *raíson d'être*.

Church documents provide the logical starting point to initiate a discussion of a Catholic school's religious mission. Figures 3a (p. 13) and 3b (p. 14) offer a chronological listing of passages from Church documents that identify the religious identity, aims, and distinctive culture of Catholic schools.

Key themes emerge. These include: an atmosphere animated by a spirit of liberty and charity based on the Gospel; a synthesis of faith and culture and faith and life; knowledge illumined by faith; the formation of a faith community; a Christian vision of the world, of life, of culture and of history; the integration of faith and reason; and, the formation of mature personalities.

These distinguishing features clearly reference the school's religious mission. At the same time, however, the documents are equally clear that this mission is not predicated solely on formal classroom religious instruction. Without doubt, the documents envision the Catholic school's religious mission from a broader context, using all-encompassing terms like "permeation," "synthesis," "integration," and "illumination" to describe this mission.

the Catholic school as a "faith community"...

One of the aims of the Catholic school is to provide an environment characterized by security and opportunity, where students feel safe to discover one's unique personhood. Though each student is made in God's image, each also possesses different needs, talents, and gifts. The Catholic school strives to draw out these gifts and to help students achieve their individual and collective potential. Experiencing success and enjoying affirmation helps build confidence, self-esteem, self-worth, and self-respect.

Faithful to the literal translation of the Latin, *Educare* ("to lead out"), the Church regards education as "the development of man from

---

Figure 3a.
The Church speaks about the religious identity, aims, and culture of Catholic schools

Declaration on Christian Education (*Gravissimum Educationis*), Vatican Council II (1965a/1996): "[The Catholic school aims] to develop in the school community an atmosphere animated by a spirit of liberty and charity based on the Gospel. It enables young people, while developing their own personalities to grow at the same time in that new life which has been given them in Baptism. Finally it so directs the whole of human culture to the message of salvation that the knowledge which the pupils acquire of the world, of life and of humanity is illumined by faith." (#8)

The Catholic School, Congregation for Catholic Education. (1977): "[T]he Catholic school has as its aim … the total formation of the individual" (#36). "These premises indicate the duties and the content of the Catholic school. Its task is fundamentally a synthesis of culture and faith, and a synthesis of faith and life: the first is reached by integrating all the different aspects of human knowledge through the subjects taught, in the light of the Gospel; the second is the growth of the virtues characteristic of the Christian." (#37)

Identify the words, phrases, or messages in these quotes that express your mission as a Catholic educational leader:

1. _____
   _____
2. _____
   _____
3. _____
   _____

---

within, freeing him from that conditioning which would prevent him from becoming a fully integrated human being" (Congregation for Catholic Education, 1977 [*The Catholic School,* hereafter referred to as *CS*], #29). If education has a liberating quality, the more integrated a person is, the less self-absorbed and better able to serve others' needs that individual will also be. The personal component of Gospel culture, then, points to the integral formation and growth of the entire human being—heart, mind, and soul.

"Gospel culture" also implies a communitarian dimension. Believing that "Christian faith, in fact, is born and grows inside a community" (*CS*, #53), the communal aspect of Catholic school education is essential to its religious mission. Well-developed community life is widely regarded as a distinguishing feature of Catholic schools, an essential ingredient for their effectiveness academically and in terms of religious formation (Coleman *et al.*, 1982, Coleman & Hoffer, 1987).

Effective Catholic Schools (Bryk, Holland, Lee, & Carriedo, 1984) spoke of Catholic identity and culture of schools in terms of the school's "Catholic character." By 1993, *Catholic Schools and the Common Good* was unequivocal: "Anyone who has recently spent time inside Catholic high schools finds it difficult to ignore the distinctive atmosphere in many of them. In seeking to understand this special character, we have concluded that the description used by both students

Identify the words, phrases, or messages in these quotes that express your mission as a Catholic educational leader:

1. _____

   _____

2. _____

   _____

3. _____

   _____

Figure 3b.

The Church speaks about the religious identity, aims, and culture of Catholic schools

The Religious Dimension of Education in a Catholic School, Congregation for Catholic Education. (1988): "From the first moment that a student sets foot in a Catholic school, he or she ought to have the impression of entering a new environment, one illumined by the light of faith, and having its own unique characteristics" (#25).

The Catholic School on the Threshold of the Third Millennium, Congregation for Catholic Education (1997/1998): "The endeavor to interweave reason and faith, which has become the heart of individual subjects, makes for unity, articulation and coordination, bringing forth within which is learned in school a Christian vision of the world, of life, of culture and of history....In the Catholic school's educational project there is no separation between time for learning and time for formation, between acquiring notions and growing in wisdom....In this perspective, in the Christian educational project all subjects collaborate, each with its own specific content, to the formation of mature personalities." (#14)

and adults—'we are community'—captures the essence of the schools' social organization" (Bryk *et al.*, p. 127).

Unlike the 1984 study, the authors identify four features that make Catholic schools "communal" organizations. These features are: clear boundaries for membership, shared beliefs, shared curricular, extracurricular, and religious activities that reinforce these shared beliefs, and a formal organizational structure of personnel who enact distinctive and extended roles.

It is noteworthy that both Coleman *et al.* (1994) and Bryk *et al.* (1993) both speak of Catholic school community in religious terms. While many private and public schools can and do build community, the distinction and added strength of community as it exists in Catholic schools is the dimension that is religious in nature and motivation. McDermott (1997) summarizes it this way: "The Catholic school is unique because it is a religious community within an academic community" (p. 11).

In essence, a "Gospel culture" is exemplified in a "faith community." In *To Teach as Jesus Did* (National Conference of Catholic Bishops, 1972), the U.S. bishops capture this notion using these words: "Community is central to educational ministry both as a necessary condition and an ardently desired goal. The educational efforts of the Church must therefore be directed to forming persons-in-community; for the education of the individual Christian is important not only to his solitary destiny but also to the destinies of the many communities in which he lives" (#13). Further, "[b]uilding and living community must be prime, explicit goals of the contemporary Catholic school" (#108).

Well-developed community life is widely regarded as the distinguishing feature of Catholic schools. But, what distinguishes these *faith* communities from their public and private counterparts is that the who, what, and why of community is intentionally connected to the Gospel, making these faith communities "Gospel cultures."

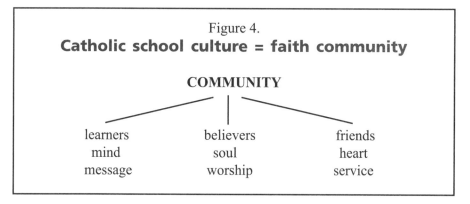

Figure 4.
Catholic school culture = faith community

COMMUNITY

learners	believers	friends
mind	soul	heart
message	worship	service

Building on this notion, one can argue that community is the basis for the entire way of life in Catholic schools—religious, academic, and social. Forming persons-in-community, then, means developing the heart, mind, and soul of students by immersing them in a community of learners, believers, and friends (Figure 4).

the Catholic school as a "culture of relationships"...

One need not look any further than the foundational belief in the Trinity to grasp the centrality of relationship in Christian theology. The three Persons are not only intimately related to each other as Father, Son and Holy Spirit. They are also triune—three Persons in one God. Jesus' teaching captures the essence of this relational mandate: "Love God above all else; love your neighbor as yourself" (Mark 12:28-31). Catholic core values like sacramentality, mediation, communion, and tradition (McBrien, 1994) underscore this notion.

Figure 5.
Catholic school culture = a culture of relationships

A relationship with .... God
.... self
.... others
........the local and world community

A relationship between........................... faith and culture
.... faith and reason
.... faith and life

Reflect upon your school's effectiveness in forming persons-in-community.
- How do you provide for the integral growth of the whole student—heart, mind, and soul?
- How do you build a community of learners, believers, and friends within your school?

Suggest three actions you will take to increase your school's effectiveness in forming persons-in-community:

1. _____
   _____
2. _____
   _____
3. _____
   _____

Of this "culture of relationships," which relationship do you believe needs strengthening in your school community?

_____

Identify what you can you do to strengthen this relationship:

_____
_____
_____
_____

Education of the entire person—the hallmark of Catholic education—encompasses not only the relationship of the student's heart, mind, and soul but also the student's relationships with God and others. It could be argued that Catholic school culture is a "culture of relationships" (Figure 5, p. 15). A school is authentically and distinctively Catholic when it fosters relationships that are both human and divine as well as when it inculcates an awareness about how knowledge, culture, faith, and human relationships find their true origin in God.

a working definition of Catholic school culture...

An inviting, supportive school culture grounded in faith community is a prerequisite for religious instruction to take hold in students' minds, hearts, and souls. However, the school's role in cultivating faith for many students might only amount to planting seeds (pre-evangelization). The taking root of faith (evangelization) and its flowering (catechesis) might occur only long after graduation.

Figure 6 provides the working definition of Catholic school culture that will be used throughout *Architects of Catholic Culture*. This definition revises and expands Flynn's (1993) definition to imply "intentionality" on the part of the Catholic educational leader. In other words, Catholic educational leaders must deliberately and consciously introduce and immerse newcomers into the culture for the purpose of passing on school culture through acculturation and socialization. Furthermore, Catholic educational leaders must deliberately and consciously renew Catholic school culture so that it remains a "living heritage," influencing daily life in the school community.

Figure 6.
A definition of Catholic school culture

Catholic school culture is...

...a "way of life" rooted in Christ, a Gospel-based creed and code, and a Catholic vision that provides inspiration and identity, is shaped over time, and is passed from one generation to the next through devices that capture and stimulate the Catholic imagination such as symbols and traditions.

Culture, then, is an organizational dynamic that Catholic educational leaders must attend to, keeping in mind the concepts of intentionality, religious mission, and Catholic imagination described in Chapter 1. Furthermore, the culture of Catholic schools—the hidden, informal curriculum—identified in Chapter 2, influences both academic and religious outcomes. Using these notions as a foundation, Chapter 3 initiates a seven-chapter exploration of an architectural plan that identifies the building blocks which Catholic educational leaders can use to build culture in Catholic schools.

• Core beliefs and values...

Core beliefs and values refer to the cherished, universally accepted ideals that groups hold in common. Taken together, core beliefs and values represent what groups stand for and aspire to as well as what groups hold sacred. These commonly accepted ideals form a collective identity as they provide meaning and evoke pride. Theorists generally agree that core values are the keystone—the foundational element—of culture. In other words, a culture is strong to the degree it is cohesive in terms of ideals.

Catholic culture...

While Catholics share many beliefs in common with other Christians, there are fundamental beliefs and values that distinguish Catholicism from other Christian denominations.

Since Vatican II, Catholic theologians have attempted to identify Catholicism's distinguishing features. Much of this work builds on that of Gilkey (1975), a Baptist theologian. McBrien (1994) has popularized Catholicism's distinguishing features, notably sacramentality, mediation, and communion, which identify how Catholics experience God and religion. McBrien argues that while Catholicism shares each of these principles with at least one other religion, it is the unique configuration of these principles that distinguishes the Catholic religious tradition. Other Catholic theologians have amended McBrien's list (Groome, 1996, 1998; Hellwig, 1995), each adding differing perspectives, emphases, and nuances.

Undergirding Catholic culture is a configuration of core beliefs and values that distinguish Catholicism from other Christian denominations. According to McBrien (1994), Hellwig (1995), and Groome (1996, 1998), Catholics acknowledge God's presence in the world and therefore view the world and life as *sacrament*, believing they can encounter God in the world through the *mediated* presence of Christ and His Church. The Catholic experience of God also occurs within *community*, a community that is *universal* and *inclusive*, which includes the communion of saints. Catholics believe that God reveals Himself through Scripture as well as through historical *tradition*. Believing in the interplay of *faith and reason*, Catholics imagine God through analogy and metaphor and experience religion through the five senses. Catholics believe in basic *human goodness*; therefore, each individual has a *personhood* deserving of dignity and respect. Because of this, Catholics believe that all people have a social responsibility to protect all human life by working for *justice*.

This composite scholarship (McBrien, 1994; Hellwig, 1995; Groome 1996, 1998), proves instructive, if not invaluable, to Catholic educational leaders in their role as architects of Catholic culture. In the final analysis, these core beliefs and values should permeate all

Surveying what theologians list as Catholic core beliefs and values, is there one Catholic core belief and value that is not present in your school and that you would like to make a priority?

_____

Identify what you can do to make this Catholic core belief and value a priority in your school:

1. _____

   _____

2. _____

   _____

3. _____

   _____

Catholic institutions, including Catholic schools.

school culture...

The opening scene of the movie *Dead Poets Society* demonstrates how a school can promote its core values. The beginning of the first assembly of the new school year features a parade of banners emblazoned with the school's values. The headmaster asks, "Gentleman, what are the four pillars?" The students then rise and respond in unison, "Tradition, Honor, Discipline, Excellence."

A Minnesota junior high school, in contrast, enshrines its six core values in a "Bill of Rights," paraphrased as follows: freedom to develop one's personality without peer pressure; freedom from physical or mental abuse; freedom from being ostracized or made fun of because of race, sex, religion, size, etc.; freedom from harassment or disrespect; and, freedom to learn without interruption (Johnston, 1995, pp. 12-13).

When it comes to core values and beliefs, the bottom line is the degree to which the core values are universally accepted and set a definitive framework for educational decision making. Many argue that one of the problems that plagues today's public schools is this lack of cohesion, or what Coleman and Hoffer (1987) call "values consistency." Logic dictates that school communities which exhibit values cohesion would have the advantages of speed and clarity in terms of daily decision making and long-term planning. The researchers cite "magnet" schools as public schools that have fostered values cohesion. As noted in Chapter 1, however, Coleman and Hoffer maintain that the values consistency of "value communities" may not be enough. What is needed in the education and formation of youth is a "functional community" possessing the "social capital" that is so influential in forming youth.

What might be the lesson for Catholic educational leaders? Although Catholic schools are touted as effective examples of both "value communities" and "functional communities," without constant attention to values socialization and community building, the social capital which has contributed so much to Catholic school effectiveness will dissipate.

Catholic school culture...

"Gospel values" is a generic term used frequently to identify the core beliefs and values of Catholic schooling and to put flesh on the way Church documents describe Catholic school culture (cf. Figures 3a & 3b, pp. 13-14). However, one cannot assume that people in Catholic schools, including some Catholic educators, know and, of greater significance to school culture, agree upon these values (Figure 7, p. 19).

Like ASCD's *What We Believe: Positions of the Association for Supervision and Curriculum Development* (Brandt, 1997), the NCEA-sponsored National Congress on Catholic Schools for the 21st

Figure 7.
Gospel values animating Catholic schooling

Faith ....truth, fidelity, tradition, doctrine, prayer, revelation, reading scripture

Service ....commitment, caring, concern, involvement, empathy, almsgiving

Courage ....sacrifice, self-denial, fortitude, restraint, discipline, patience, temperance

Justice ....courage, risk, human dignity, stewardship, prophecy, interdependence, peace-seeking, equal distribution of goods, fortitude, empathy

Hope ....optimism, confidence, joy, realism, providence, trust, prophecy

Love ....(towards God) – reverence, worship, submission, prayer; (towards self) – self-esteem, prudence, temperance, creativity; (toward others) – care, concern, respect, acceptance

Reconciliation ....forgiveness, mercy, compassion, humility, conflict resolution, work to eliminate evil, love of enemy

Community ....personal dignity, belonging, equality, fellowship, trust, care

Source: Reck, C. (1983). *Vision and Values*. Washington, DC: National Catholic Educational Association

Identify the Gospel value or charism you believe should be emphasized in your school:

_____

How might you connect this Gospel value or charism more explicitly with your school's religious mission?

_____
_____
_____
_____

Cite what you might do to strengthen this connection:

1. _____
_____
2. _____
_____
3. _____
_____

Century (1992) developed a list of belief statements regarding the Catholic identity of Catholic schools. These statements emphasize values such as community, celebration, worship, service, integration of faith and reason, human dignity, and spirituality. Notably, the statements also include values such as academic excellence and intellectual growth which are not necessarily religious in nature but have nonetheless become essential elements in the broader interpretation of Catholic identity.

For schools sponsored by the Church's religious congregations, core beliefs and values often reflect the charism of the sponsoring religious community, ascribing particular meaning to these core beliefs and values. Jesuit schools, for example, stress reflection and service to others in keeping with the Ignatian tradition of being "contemplatives in action," "men and women for others," and "leaders in service." Schools sponsored by the Sisters of Mercy list as two of their core values "compassion and service" as well as "concern for women and women's issues," which have deep roots in the Mercy tradition inspired by Venerable Catherine McCauley. The Ursuline Campus Schools (Louisville, KY), express four core values, namely, community, leadership, reverence, and service emanating from the Ursuline charism and

Saint Angela Merici. The Network of Sacred Heart Schools operate out of a set of principles that have characterized Sacred Heart education since the Society of Sacred Heart's founding by Saint Madeleine Sophie Barat. These principles include: "personal and active faith in God, a deep respect for intellectual values, and personal growth in an atmosphere of wise freedom."

While Catholic schools share certain beliefs and values in common with public schools, such as community service and academic excellence, the synonyms invoked when describing Catholic school culture imply that religious principles—not civic virtues—motivate Catholic schooling. A public school might see as its ultimate goal to graduate persons of virtue. By contrast, a Catholic school "transforms a [person] of virtue into a [person] of Christ" (Congregation for Catholic Education, 1977, #47). Given this, the primary duty of the Catholic educational leader—as an architect of Catholic culture—is to connect the school's core values and beliefs to Christ and the Gospel intentionally, deliberately, and continually.

Authentic Catholic schools exude a Gospel culture, that is, they are faith communities that intentionally connect what they do with the Gospel. Furthermore, Catholic educational leaders—as architects of Catholic culture—must actively socialize the school community to build values cohesion and a web of support that functions as social capital (Coleman *et al.*, 1982; Coleman & Hoffer, 1987).

"Respect" has been suggested by some practitioners as a starting point because it is an overarching value which encompasses many other values. Research (Coleman *et al.*, 1982; Coleman & Hoffer, 1987; Bryk & Driscoll, 1988; Bryk *et al.*, 1993) suggests that the core value of "community" might be a place to start. Echoing Maslow (1970), the *National Catechetical Directory* (National Conference of Catholic Bishops, 1979) acknowledges "belonging" as one of several basic human needs that might require to be satisfied to "prepare the ground for the gospel message" (#34). It would seem then that building "community" is a pre-condition for building a "faith community," characterized by the core values of "message," "service," and "worship." Put simply, there cannot be faith community until there is community first (Figure 4, p. 15).

"Relationships" may be an additional core value that undergirds many others. If Catholic school culture is a "culture of relationships" (Figure 5, p. 15), then relationships provide a unifying theme subsuming many other core values and may even be considered a precondition for community. Only through the building of relationships, in particular, and the building of community, in general, will people in Catholic schools actively construct a faith community.

CULTURAL BUILDING PLAN:
IDENTIFY AND INTEGRATE CORE BELIEFS & VALUES
USING THE MISSION STATEMENT AND RESOURCES

To ascertain just what a school's core values are—what is sacred—Catholic educational leaders should initiate some collective "soul searching" (Cook, 1999, p. 22).

As architects of Catholic culture, Catholic educational leaders should identify core values, explicitly connecting them to the Gospel and religious mission. Principals can do this by linking the school's mission statement, which is the singular official document that identifies precisely what the school holds sacred, with the school's allocation of resources, financial and otherwise, which demonstrate concretely what the school considers sacred (Cook, 1998, 1999).

A School's Mission Statement:
Clarifying Identity, Inspiration, and Destiny

A Catholic school mission statement encapsulates and clarifies its identity, inspiration, and destiny. It captures the school's essence and it serves as a compass to direct daily life in schools. The school's mission statement is the keystone, lending stability to the whole structure.

- *Identity*: The Catholic's school mission statement identifies the school community and explains its purpose. The mission statement also pinpoints the school's core values as well as its non-negotiables.
- *Inspiration*: The Catholic school's mission statement articulates its meaning and purpose. An effective mission statement generates excitement, inspires passion, and galvanizes commitment by challenging the community to aspire to cherished ideals. At the same time, the mission statement reassures and provides stability and continuity.
- *Destiny*: The mission statement, or an addendum, announces the school's goals. It provides a vision of what the school community aspires to become. The mission statement enables the school to stay on course in its decisions, actions, behaviors, and activities.

Identity, inspiration, and destiny are rooted in culture and should be integrated into a school's mission statement. At San Xavier Mission School (Tucson, AZ), the mission statement is built around the faith of the tohono O'odham people which has nurtured a Christian spirit and Catholic belief since the days of Father Eusebio Kino, who began this mission. Similarly, the mission statement at St. Mary Mission School (Red Lake, MN) is rooted in Ojibwe culture. One way Ojibwe

Read your school's mission statement. Check all questions the statement answers:

____ *Who are we?*
____ *Why do we exist?*
____ *How are we unique?*
____ *What do we do?*
____ *Who do we serve?*
____ *What inspires us?*
____ *Who do we hope to become?*
____ *What do we stand for?*

Does your mission statement refer to:

____ *God?*
____ *Jesus?*
____ *the Church?*
____ *Does your mission statement use the word "Catholic"?*
____ *Does your mission statement clearly distinguish your mission as a Catholic school from the missions of public, independent, and other denominational schools?*
____ *Can students or faculty recite or paraphrase your school's mission statement?*

Review your check marks. Specify the message that your school's mission statement actually sends:

_____

_____

_____

_____

cultural values manifest themselves at St. Mary is the ongoing effort at non-violent conflict resolution, especially by engaging in eye-to-eye processes when conflicts arise.

A Catholic school's mission statement, then, defines, inspires, and guides the school community in all it does. The Catholic school's identity, inspiration, and destiny—as expressed in a mission statement—must then be explicitly connected to Christ and the Gospel (National Conference of Catholic Bishops, 1972, #155).

When mission statements truly drive the schooling enterprise, learning activities and outcomes will look very different (Figure 8).

Figure 8.
Comparing mission statements

Dayton (OH) Public Schools: The mission of the Dayton Public Schools, as the transforming agent of the community, is to guarantee all students 100 percent success through a network of independent competing instructional services that actualize the unique potential of each person. (Cook, 1990, p. 184)

Des Moines (IA) Catholic Schools: The mission of the Catholic schools of the Diocese of Des Moines is to provide meaningful educational experiences for children/adolescents in an environment integrated by Gospel values which nurture faith, community, prayer and service. (L. Gubbels, Superintendent of Schools, personal communication, August 26, 1999)

Unfortunately, however, some Catholic school mission statements are general and vague, almost non-committal. The litmus test of a Catholic school's mission statement is this: Can people tell that the school is Catholic by reading its mission statement?

Displaying the Mission Statement

When the mission statement serves as the keystone of a school's cultural architecture, it should be showcased at every opportunity.

At St. Cyril School (Tucson, AZ), the mission statement is painted on the school office wall for everyone who enters to read. The statement is printed in the parent/student handbook and in the teacher handbook. It is discussed at the annual visitation day for families interested in the school. The implementation of the mission statement is described at the beginning of the academic year at the back-to-school parent meetings. During Catholic Schools Week, the principal describes the mission statement in a parish bulletin article. In addition, the mission statement is presented at every Mass on School Sunday. The teachers post the mission statement in their classrooms and teach it every year to their students. At the orientation program for school board members, the principal explains the mission statement. Lastly, whenever any new program or activity is being considered, the mission statement is used as an evaluative criterion.

Integrating the Mission Statement

It is not enough to write a mission statement and display it. A mission statement must breathe life into curriculum, instruction, and activities as well as drive educational decision making. The ultimate goal for any Catholic school is to be mission-driven rather than crisis-driven. Synonyms like infusion, permeation, and embeddedness indicate that full integration occurs in levels, degrees, and stages.

• *continuous referencing*

As architects of Catholic culture, it is incumbent upon Catholic educational leaders to keep core values and the mission statement in front of their school communities. One way to draw attention to the mission statement is to reference it in prayer and speeches.

As a means of keeping the school community's mission in mind, the principal of St. Raphael School (Louisville, KY) includes reading the mission statement in the prayer at the beginning of each faculty meeting.

The mission statement for Nativity School (Columbus, OH) proclaims: "Nativity provides a program of solid academic instruction with a global perspective that is enriched by the arts and rooted in the gospel." The principal utilizes the four headings/areas (academics, global education, the arts, religious education/service) to form outlines for presentations, remarks, and reports given at School Committee, PTA, Parish Council, and Faculty meetings.

At Christ the King School (Daphne, AL), the principal is not the only person who references the school mission statement: "Our mission statement summarizes the reason for the school's existence and the faculty, staff, and students all memorize it. Not only can the students recite it, they also can explain what it means in action" (M. Nolan, personal communication, January, 1997).

• *themes*

Many Catholic educational leaders use the core values and beliefs as themes for individual projects or all school activities during a certain time frame. Figure 9 (p. 25) shows a thematic approach to mission integration.

• *course unit on mission statement*

Another approach to mission integration is to make the study of the mission statement a discrete unit in the religion curriculum. At

Mount Carmel Academy (New Orleans, LA), the students study the purpose of the school and mission statement in a unit of ninth grade religion. "We are still working to integrate it into the other activities. We hope that, with faculty involvement in performing skits and making presentations to one another concerning our mission statement and our behavior together as Catholic educators, it will become easier for teachers to incorporate the mission statement more actively in their curriculum" (C. A. Campbell, personal communication, January, 1997).

> *Cite three ways your school's mission statement is integrated into its "way of life":*
>
> 1. _____
> 2. _____
> 3. _____
>
> *Suggest three additional ways to integrate the school's mission and/or mission statement into its "way of life":*
>
> 1. _____
>   _____
> 2. _____
>   _____
> 3. _____
>   _____

• *discipline*

At Christ the King (Daphne, AL), the mission statement serves as the point of reference for student discipline: "Our faculty are very conscious of the importance of our mission statement and refer to it in all areas of our life. When I encounter any discipline problem I always ask, 'Would you do that to Jesus Christ?' Students usually stop and reflect for a moment and answer, 'No.' I often ask them to write the mission statement in their own words and to tell me how they can live it out in their daily actions" (M. Nolan, personal communication, January, 1997).

Writing Corollary and Follow-up Documents

Going hand-in-hand with mission integration is writing follow-up documents that elaborate the core values and beliefs stated in the school's mission statement. Some school communities look at core values in terms of what attitudes and behaviors a typical graduate should possess and exhibit. Jesuit schools, like Creighton Prep (Omaha, NE), base corollary documents on the "Profile of the Graduate of a Jesuit High School at Graduation" published by the Jesuit Secondary Education Association (The Commission on Research and Development, 1981/1994). The Curriculum Committee at V. J. and Angela Skutt Catholic High School (Omaha, NE) wrote a similar document called "Graduation Outcomes." The Institute for Catholic Education in Ontario, Canada, used a system-wide approach to formulate "Expectations of the Ontario Catholic School Graduate."

The principal of St. Gabriel School (San Francisco, CA) offers this suggestion: "We have produced a booklet to describe the practical ways in which our mission statement is reflected in the school program. The statement is analyzed and applied sentence by sentence. This booklet has been distributed to our parents, parish community, visitors to the school, and friends. It has been very useful in drawing attention to our mission statement and to point out the ways in which we integrate our mission statement into all facets of school life" (M. P. Borghello, personal communication, January, 1997).

Figure 9.
A thematic approach to mission integration

St. Albert the Great Catholic School (Reno, NV):

At St. Albert's School, the faculty selects a "theme" word for the school year. This theme follows the mission statement and is incorporated into all aspects of daily life both in and out of school. The word for the year is displayed throughout the school and classrooms as well as in newsletters, marketing releases, and in various prominent places in the school and parish. The yearly theme is broken down into a word for each month.

One year, the theme was "Christian."

<u>C</u>hristlike	<u>I</u>nspirational	<u>I</u>ntegrity
<u>H</u>umble	<u>S</u>incere	<u>A</u>ttitude
<u>R</u>esponsible	<u>T</u>rustworthy	<u>N</u>eighborly

The word for the month of September was Christ-like. During September, the faculty discussed definitions of Christ-like and identified Christ-like behaviors. Each grade then incorporated the word and behavior into various lessons throughout the month.

When the school community gathered each morning, a student would share a Christ-like behavior observed the previous day. This pattern continued throughout each month with each new word, beginning with a definition of the word and the behavior that each member of the school community could incorporate into daily life.

At the monthly Parent Teacher Organization meeting, each grade took a turn presenting a short skit, song, poem, etc., utilizing the word of the month. This allowed the students a chance to show their families what they are learning and incorporating into their daily lives.

The first Wednesday of each month featured an "Honors Assembly." At this assembly, two students from each grade were selected by their peers and honored for the Christian character they exhibited. Photographs were taken for the yearbook and the students were given a free dress pass, a free dinner from one of the local restaurants, and a pin (reading "Excellence") to wear on their uniform.

Assessing the Mission in Light of the Mission Statement

Unfortunately, many school communities are energetic at the goal-setting stage but tired when it comes time for self-evaluation. What can a Catholic educational leader do to reduce this human and institutional tendency?

In terms of structures, many schools have a school board standing committee whose charge is to assess school programs and directions through the lens of mission. At Mater Dei High School (Breese, IL), the committee is the Mission Effectiveness Committee. Charged with evaluating how well the school community lives out the mission statement, this committee identifies specific goals for the year and continuously assesses the degree to which each goal is being achieved.

In terms of processes, many Catholic educational leaders report that reflecting upon the mission statement is a natural and ongoing aspect of educational decision making. The principal of Parkersburg Catholic High School (Parkersburg, WV) illustrates this notion: "The Gospels tell many beautiful stories of people with physical and mental problems who seek Jesus' help and experience His warm and loving response to their requests. In 1991, Parkersburg Catholic High School recognized that the mission of our school was incomplete without the active acceptance of this message. Starting with the goal of full inclusion of all students into our classrooms, a 'special needs' program was developed. Through a significant budgetary commitment, grants, and voluntary efforts, we now have over 30 students enrolled in the program. The school is ADA accessible and many voluntary service hours are dedicated to those special people Jesus loved and healed. The school, through budget expenditures and hands-on experience, has enhanced its religious mission and raised the spiritual level of the entire school community" (M. R. Hattman, personal communication, January, 1997).

Commit Resources to the Religious Mission of the School

"Put your money where your mouth is" is the quintessential challenge people issue when they want words translated into effective action.

Discussing how to assess and transform school culture, Maehr and Buck (1993) identify how resource allocation signals a school's values. In their succinct terms, "Budgets reflect goals; expenditures reflect values" (p. 49). As these authors envision this phenomenon, it is the allocation of resources, not the mission statement, which reveals more about what a school community values in practice. "Teachers and students are sensitive to how resources are allocated, particularly since most schools operate on limited budgets, and in this way come to understand what is valued and not valued in the school" (p. 50).

The "bottom line" question for Catholic educational leaders—as architects of Catholic culture—focuses upon the percentage of the school budget that is directed toward programs that implement the school's religious mission. O'Malley (1991) bluntly asks: "Is your retreat budget as large as your athletic budget?" (p. 8). At Creighton Prep (Omaha, NE), the school's most recent multi-year capital campaign designated "Jesuit identity" as one of the campaign's focal points. School leaders earmarked a portion of the fund drive appeal for programs that support the school's religious mission.

While Maehr and Buck equate resources with money, a broader

Describe a recent situation in which you evaluated a school program, activity, direction, or issue in light of the mission statement:

_____

_____

_____

_____

_____

What current issue in your school do you believe needs to be decided in light of mission?

_____

_____

Identify actions you might take to ensure that this issue is decided in light of the school's mission:

1. _____

_____

2. _____

_____

3. _____

_____

definition of resources is in order. This is especially true given that the National Conference of Catholic Bishops speaks about stewardship of resources in terms of "time, talent, and treasure" (1993, p. 45). Where Catholic schools are concerned, resources refer not only to money but also to personnel, space, time, and energy.

• personnel

Catholic schools must have personnel capable of carrying forward the school's religious mission. Take teachers of religion, for instance. Even though it is rare for a Catholic school principal to hire non-certified teachers to teach secular subjects, there is good reason to question whether teachers of religion have adequate educational background and/or training in the field. A full one-fifth of elementary school religion teachers have no formal credential for teaching religion. Another one-fifth are currently enrolled in courses (Galetto, 1996). Anecdotal evidence suggests a similar situation exists at the secondary level.

Besides having qualified religion instructors, additional staff may be necessary to implement and bear responsibility for other aspects of the school's religious mission. Campus ministers, for example, have become increasingly common. These women and men perform duties for which a full-time religion teacher would have little time, such as planning liturgies and coordinating student and faculty retreats. In those schools with very sophisticated and extensive Christian student service programs, a full-time person coordinates these programs.

A small number of Catholic high schools have created a second-tier administrative post for the purpose of attending to the religious mission of the school in a more deliberate and systematic way. At Magnificat High School (Rocky River, OH), the Director of Mission Effectiveness fulfills this role. Responsible to the president and principal, the Director promotes the values of the school's Mission and Philosophy with the goal that every member of the school community be able to name the essential elements of the Mission and to articulate its manifestations in their areas. As a member of the school's administrative team, the Director also evaluates mission effectiveness annually with faculty, staff, students, parents, and alumnae. Lastly, the Director educates new faculty and staff about the history and heritage of Magnificat High School and the Community of the Sisters of the Humility of Mary.

• time

Time is a valuable commodity and jockeying for time in schools is as old as the schooling enterprise itself. But, as schools are required to provide new services inside the classroom and out, the number of competing interests has exploded.

In Catholic schools, the issue is even more pronounced given the school's religious dimension. Minimally, time must be set aside for religious instruction. Decisions about the amount of time devoted

Identify the percentage of the school budget devoted to:

____ % *Academics*
____ % *Athletics*
____ % *Liturgies/Retreats*
_100_ %

What, if anything, does this suggest about your school's budgeting priorities?

_____
_____
_____
_____

Identify how any imbalance between the school's mission and its budgeting priorities might be redressed:

1. _____
   _____
2. _____
   _____
3. _____
   _____

Effective faith formation programs require staff adequate for the need. Check which of the following staff members your school needs in order to boast about an effective faith formation program:

___ *Religion teacher(s)*
___ *Campus minister(s)*
___ *Christian Service Coordinator*
___ *Director of Mission Effectiveness*

Other(s):

___ _____
___ _____
___ _____
___ _____
___ _____
___ _____

to religious instruction send subtle messages about how it is valued not only as an academic subject, but also how it is valued in light of the school's larger purpose.

Core values also dictate that the school community will use time for other religious activities, like school liturgies and student and faculty retreats. Weekly mass may be embraced in one school, but not in another. At Mercy High School (Omaha, NE), in addition to the mandatory monthly liturgy, the principal sets aside one class period each week for Mass, which is optional for students. Usually two-thirds of the student body attends this Mass, while the remaining students report to study hall. Time taken from instruction for student retreats can become a point of contention. Yet, more often than not, it might not be retreats that are the problem but the way retreats are scheduled. Scheduling retreats in a way that minimizes disruptions might be the only solution necessary to reconcile the integrity of the retreat program with academic concerns.

The principal of St. Stephen School (San Francisco, CA) places a premium on time set aside for retreats, in this case, faculty retreats: "In planning the school calendar each year, a staff day is set aside to bring the teachers together to pray. Each spring the teachers and staff are invited to 'come away' and spend a day relating on a deeper level with their God and with each other. This day takes different forms each year and, after seeking input from the staff as to their needs and desires, this special time is planned. An inspirational place is secured and all come together for talks, quiet time for prayer, and liturgy. The day always includes a meal where teachers and staff can share..." (P. Simms, personal communication, January, 1997).

• *energy*

Closely akin to the issue of time is energy. Neither humans nor human institutions can devote equal energy to everything. In view of the fact that human energy is a finite resource, choices about where a school will focus its energy reveal a value system. Since a leader's personality and authority influences organizational priorities, it is the Catholic educational leader's duty to keep religious mission in front of the school community so that human energy is spent wisely.

There are different approaches Catholic educational leaders can take in order to steer human energy in the direction of religious mission.

For example, St. Ignatius School (Mobile, AL) sponsored a 2-day convocation involving over 200 members of the community as a culmination of its long-range strategic planning process. One of the nine areas of study was the school's spiritual life. The convocation produced four goals: assure academic excellence in religious education; encourage parental involvement in religious education; provide advanced training in theology for teachers; enhance the spirituality of the whole community. In addition, the convocation identified seven priorities:

liturgy; curriculum; sacramental preparation; community outreach; spiritual/moral development; staff education/formation; student ministry. From these priorities, the convocation formulated 16 sub-goals.

At Sacred Heart School (West Des Moines, IA), a team of teachers assists the principal in planning staff development programs. One year, the team focused on Eucharist. The parish Director of Religious Education met bimonthly with the religion teachers. Also, the pastor assisted in staff development by training the entire staff as Eucharistic ministers during an in-service meeting. The principal concludes: "We believe that every person at Sacred Heart School is a teacher of religion whether they actually teach the class or not. Ongoing faith formation for staff is a high priority of the school staff development team" (A. Westerhaus, personal communication, January, 1997).

• *space*

The way space is allocated sends a message about what the Catholic school reveres. How the school's sacred space compares with it labs or sports facilities reflects priorities. An unused chapel or one that doubles as a classroom reflects priorities.

The location of the chapel and/or campus ministry office sends a message, intended or not. Creighton Prep (Omaha, NE) prioritized the relocation of the Campus Ministry Office in a recent capital building project. "When we built our 2.3 million-dollar student commons in 1991, we placed priority on mission when weighing building priorities. Since the use of resources ultimately communicates what an institution values, we wanted our message to be clear. Therefore, when building the student commons, we chose to place the Campus Ministry Office at the physical center of student activity at Prep. Because the students' spiritual development stands at the core of our Jesuit identity, we wanted this priority to be clear in the layout of our new building. Now every student passes by the spiritual nerve center of our school several times per day. We hope this subtle reminder helps students begin to understand the importance of faith in their lives. Because of campus ministry's location, students are more apt to get involved in the worship, service, and retreat opportunities campus ministry sponsors. In the end, our architectural priorities have helped us stay true to who we are as a Jesuit school" (D. J. Fraynd, personal communication, July, 1999).

The principal of Mount Carmel Academy (New Orleans, LA) suggests that any space can be transformed into a sacred space: "Although our chapel is not yet a reality, plans are underway for its completion. In the meantime, our faith community at Mount Carmel Academy is so strong that we can create a spiritual setting in all areas of our school. One day the gym is a gym, the next day it is the setting for Mass. One day the Performing Arts Center provides the stage for a play, the next day it is the setting for the Stations of the Cross and a prayer service.

Review your school's budget and strategic plan.

Check which budget items indicating the priority given to your school's religious mission:
___ *staffing*
___ *retreats*
___ *liturgies/worship*
___ *faculty faith formation*

other(s):
___ _____
___ _____
___ _____
___ _____

Check which strategic plan items indicate the priority given to your school's religious mission:
___ *build a school chapel*
___ *hire campus minister(s)*

other(s):
___ _____
___ _____

In light of these priorities, identify how you will devote adequate school resources to your school's religious mission:

1. _____
_____
2. _____
_____
3. _____
_____

Our new chapel will be wonderful once finished, but it will only add to the sacred spaces we have created throughout our campus. We try to make God an evident force in all that we experience at Mount Carmel Academy" (C. A. Campbell, personal communication, January, 1997).

The Interplay of Money, Personnel, Time, Space, and Energy

Since money, personnel, time, space, and energy are finite resources, choices must be made. As architects of Catholic culture, Catholic educational leaders serve as chief stewards of the school's resources by considering their school's religious mission and core values when allocating resources. Furthermore, given an atmosphere of competing and worthwhile interests and needs, it is incumbent upon Catholic educational leaders to educate their school communities about the necessity of giving religious mission priority in strategic planning efforts and subsequent budget decisions.

When faced with the facts of the school budget, some principals contend that money is the bottom line for assessing what a school values. Money, however, is not the bottom line. Instead, choice and the values embodied in each choice provide the bottom line. This is significant in view of the pivotal role that Catholic educational leaders play in decision making. In this case, the question focuses upon whether and to what degree Catholic educational leaders will endeavor to earmark resources for efforts that further their school's religious mission.

Chapter Summary

Core beliefs and values refer to cherished ideals that a group holds in common. They provide collective identity and meaning. Core beliefs and values serve as the foundational element of cultural architecture. A culture is strong to the degree that there is cohesiveness and commitment about group ideals and purpose.

The Catholic school is an expression of the educational mission of the Church. Therefore, Catholic educational leaders must ensure that Catholic core convictions and Gospel values, and perhaps the charism of a religious congregation, form the foundation for the Catholic school way of life.

As architects of Catholic culture, Catholic educational leaders emphasize their school's mission statement by displaying it, by referencing it continuously, by integrating it into all school activities and decisions, as well as by assessing programs and the school's way of life in light of the core beliefs and values contained in the mission statement. As stewards of limited financial resources, Catholic educational leaders see to it that the allocation of these resources gives top priority to the school's religious mission.

Chapter 4

• Heroes and heroines ...

Through their words and actions, individuals can exemplify a group's core values. These may be expressed in the form of character traits, personal qualities, what Deal and Kennedy call the "right stuff" (1982, p. 37). These core values may also be evidenced in an individual's accomplishments reflecting group values.

Living or deceased, these exemplars perform an invaluable function. They are the women and men who others relate to or identify with, epitomize all that is good about a culture, and demonstrate what it takes to be an exemplary citizen. Heroes and heroines set high standards; their lives challenge others to attain those standards. In the final analysis, heroes and heroines are role models others can emulate.

Catholic culture...

The pantheon of Catholic heroes and heroines is filled with paragons of Christian virtue and Christ-like behavior. Although saints appear larger than life, most were ordinary people who led extraordinary lives. Because saints come in all human shapes and sizes, there is a saint every Catholic can identify with or relate to. Augustine, Francis of Assisi, Benedict, Catherine of Siena, Ignatius of Loyola, John Neumann, Elizabeth Ann Seton, Paul Miki, Maria Goretti, John Baptiste de LaSalle and Dominic Savio represent saints of different ages, walks of life, politics, and stories. Besides canonized saints, there are other Catholics, both living and deceased, who are exemplars of Christian life, including Dorothy Day, Mother Teresa, Kateri Tekakwitha, Catherine McAuley, Oscar Romero, Pope John XXIII, and Pope John Paul II.

school culture...

Schools have heroes and heroines, like a founder, namesake, or teachers, who embody the school's ideals and are worthy of imitation. Invariably, younger students hold older students in high regard.

Who and what a school honors and rewards provide telltale signs about a school's values. Common reward mechanisms include the Honor Roll, Student of the Week, varsity letters, yearbook dedications, named buildings/facilities, faculty promotions, alumni awards, and a "wall of fame." Awards bestowed at graduation provide an unambiguous sign of what the school values. The description of this award and the selection criteria and process lay bare the school's core values.

Catholic school culture...

Because this is an age in which the society confers mega-status upon its superstars according to their degree of outrageousness and because youth are bombarded with negative influences and role models at this impressionable age, schools must promote positive role models for youth. Unlike their secular colleagues, however, Catholic educational leaders have the added challenge of promoting—in an intentional way—counter-cultural role models who personify Gospel values.

CULTURAL BUILDING PLAN:
HONOR HEROES & HEROINES WHO EXEMPLIFY GOSPEL VALUES AND RELIGIOUS MISSION

Catholic educational leaders must take the lead in identifying, promoting, and celebrating exemplars who embody the school's core values, especially Gospel-related ones. A quick way to identify and assess a school's current pool of heroes and heroines in light of core values is to contemplate the following two questions: *Who* is *honored* at your school? *What* is *rewarded* at your school?

In response to the first question, there are many role models for Catholic school leaders to identify, promote, and celebrate. These exemplars personify core values and religious mission.

Heroic Role Models (Who is honored?)

- *Jesus*: Both divine and human, Jesus is the perfect man. During His life on earth, Jesus experienced a wide range of human emotions including joy, suffering, friendship, rage, love, reluctance, confusion, struggle, courage, and temptation. Jesus' mission was to teach by word and example how to love God, neighbor, and self. Jesus—the perfect man—is the perfect hero (Vatican Council II, 1965d/1996; Congregation for Catholic Education, 1977).

- *Mary*: Conceived without original sin, Mary's life illustrates unflinching faith, purity, steadfast support, and courage. Despite her fears and doubts, Mary responded to God's call "I am the servant of the Lord. Let it be done to me as you say" (Luke 1:26-38). An exemplar of love and fidelity, Mary models what it means to respond fully to God's call.

- *Saints*: The communion of saints offers heroes and heroines representing every race, color, profession, and circumstance. For Catholic educators, exemplars include St. John Baptist de La Salle and St. Elizabeth Ann Seton. For students, the communion of saints includes Catholic youth whose lives exemplified heroic virtues, including St. Agnes (virginity, courage, calmness), St. Dominic Savio (kindness, cheerfulness, purity of heart, devotion), St. Joan of Arc (energetic spirit, bravery, hope, sense of mission), St. Maria Goretti (chastity, forgiveness, fortitude, innocence), and Blessed Pier Giorgio Frassati (devotion, service, leadership, zeal) (*Saints and Feast Days*, 1985; Kealey, 1987).

Catholic educational leaders can promote saints and other religious heroes as role models in many ways.

Identify three ways your school community honors Jesus:

1. _____
2. _____
3. _____

Discuss how you honor Mary at your school:

_____

_____

_____

Cite three additional ways your school community might honor Jesus and Mary:

1. _____
2. _____
3. _____

Anticipating All Saints Day, the seniors at Bishop Ryan High School (Minot, ND) write research papers about a particular saint and put together an authentic costume of the assigned saint. At the All Saints Day liturgy, the seniors participate in the entrance procession and, immediately following the entrance song, each "saint" is introduced and briefly explains why he or she is honored. Following the liturgy, the seniors proceed to the two Catholic elementary schools, where the younger students experience awe at seeing the "big kids" dressed as saints.

At other schools, including St. Boniface School and St. Andrew School (Erie, PA), students study the lives of the saints within a larger unit focusing upon "Heroes." One year, St. Boniface School used this theme for the entire year. In keeping with the theme, seventh-graders studied the saints as part of a month-long project in their religion and English classes. At St. Andrew School, a three-week thematic unit involved the entire student body. Each class chose a hero to research and, in religion class, students learned about the saints, bible characters, and other religious heroes. In the middle of their study, the Bishop of Erie celebrated liturgy with the children, speaking about these religious heroes and how the students can be like the saints. The Mayor of Erie came to talk as well. She spoke of the importance of religious heroes and parents as role models.

Some schools celebrate popular feast days. At Sacred Heart High School (East Grand Forks, MN), students annually celebrate the feast of St. Nicholas. One student dresses up and visits each classroom in the local Catholic elementary schools. St. Nick answers questions about himself while his helpers distribute candy canes.

Regarding the celebration of feast days, St. Cecilia School (Omaha, NE) provides an example. The principal writes: "On the feasts of St. Dominic and St. Thomas Aquinas—significant because of our Dominican heritage—some symbolic gift is given to each child, be it a holy card of Dominic or a picture, medal, etc. When any big feast arrives, we celebrate it in each room, using the *Children's Daily Prayer Book*..." (B. Pryor, personal communication, January, 1997).

Some school leaders highlight religious heroes and heroines by naming buildings and campus landmarks after these people. The architectural design of The Prout School (Wakefield, RI) is such that outdoor courtyards stand at the center of the school's three wings. When the courtyards were refurbished, each was dedicated to a Catholic hero or heroine representing a different culture—St. Francis of Assisi (European), St. Paul Miki (Japanese), and Blessed Kateri Tekakwitha (Native American). Today, the courtyards symbolically reinforce the Church's global and multicultural heritage.

While the preceding illustrations speak of Catholic heroes and heroines, Catholic educational leaders would be remiss if they did not

Name three saints/religious/heroes/heroines your school honors:

1. _____
2. _____
3. _____

Describe how these saints/religious/heroes/heroines are honored:

_____
_____
_____

Identify three additional saints/religious/heroes/heroines your school might honor:

1. _____
2. _____
3. _____

draw attention to non-Catholic exemplars like Martin Luther King and Mahatma Gandhi.

- *The School Patron or Namesake*: In view of the fact that most Catholic schools are named after saints or other religious heroes, shining the spotlight on this hero or heroine has special significance. If a school is named after a local bishop or benefactor, the school should hold up that person as a role model. These days it is common for schools sponsored by religious communities to celebrate the feast of the founder/foundress of the sponsoring religious community.

Some Catholic schools, however, are not named for a patron saint. One such school, Bishop McGuinness High School (Oklahoma City, OK) did something about this.

Believing that the students would identify more easily with a young person who lived a full but saintly life, the Director of Pastoral Care proposed in 1995 that the student body elect a youthful patron. Eventually, the administration proposed a slate of eight sainted or beatified candidates, each of whom the students studied prior to voting. One of the candidates was Pier Giorgio Frassati. Born in 1901 near Turin, Italy, he died in 1924 from polio contracted while working with the poor. During his short life, Pier Giorgio studied hard, spent many hours serving the poor, and yet he also found time to pursue his athletic interests, the foremost of which was mountain climbing. Pier Giorgio serves as an excellent role model because, like most high schoolers, he struggled to succeed scholastically even though academics did not come easily to him. More importantly though, Pier Giorgio's devotion to God, love of neighbor, and living faith serve as an excellent example for youth. Today, the Bishop McGuinness school community invokes Pier Giorgio's name at the conclusion of every moment of prayer and worship: "Blessed Pier Giorgio. Pray for us! Where are we going? Toward the Top!" The last acclamation comes from a photograph of Pier Giorgio climbing up a mountainside. Pier Giorgio wrote "Toward the Top" across his back of his shirt to encourage those who were following him. Now, the school has embraced Pier Giorgio's phrase as its motto.

- *Alumni/ae:* Students are especially drawn to past graduates because of the bond created by a shared experience. Role models who sat in the same desks, had the same teachers, and wore the same uniform are easy for students to relate to and identify with.

Other schools honor alumni/ae who are "living saints." The principal of Blessed Sacrament School (Alexandria, VA) explains how this school honors its living saints:

Identify the name of your school's patron/namesake:

_____

Discuss how the charism of the school's patron/namesake exemplifies Gospel values:

_____

_____

_____

_____

Cite what you might do to honor your patron/namesake in light of your school's religious mission:

1. _____
2. _____
3. _____

Each year we ask our hero/heroine to visit the school during Catholic Schools Week and tell his/her Catholic "faith story" and the role Blessed Sacrament School played in it. These faith stories have been profound and inspiring for both faculty and staff over the years.

One year our honoree told the students about his seventh grade basketball team and two new members who were African-Americans. These two boys were exceptional players and the team was fired up for the season. However, on the day of the first game, the coach informed the team that since the public schools were not yet integrated, the boys could not play in the league. Our hero became choked up as he told the students how terrible he felt as he watched the two African-American boys leave the team room and head home. He shared how that experience altered his perspective forever and, as an adult, he wished the team had waived playing in the county league that year. This humble hero reminded us of our Gospel call to justice and respect for all. His is a faith story we will be telling again and again.

Another year our heroine told us about the many traditions and school activities which were part of her experience in the 1950s. She spoke of students attending early morning Mass and receiving delicious sweet rolls afterwards and wearing sweaters with embroidered hearts with crosses, representing the Sisters of the Holy Cross who founded the school. This alumna's talk helped us to appreciate the richness of our Catholic faith history as well as the heroines who built a strong foundation for our Catholic school. (M. Dowling, personal communication, June, 1999)

- *Teachers*: Educators are "heroes in our midst" whose heroism oftentimes remains unsung. Catholic Schools Week provides an excellent opportunity to honor educators. What is important to remember is to connect teacher recognition to core values and religious mission.
- *Students*: There are no better role models for students than one another.

The principal at Monte Cassino (Tulsa, OK) encourages students to honor each other as living saints:

The heroes celebrated at Monte Cassino are both living and deceased. Students have a great knowledge and respect for the lives of the saints. They enjoy dressing as and reporting on favorite saints. They also celebrate living saints among themselves—fellow students or teachers whose everyday lives remind them of Gospel living. Through "student of the week," classroom "May Children" and newsletter accounts, students are affirmed in their acts of charity. When one of the second grade students died suddenly of lung cancer, the students, parents, and teachers grieved together, honoring this young boy's goodness through stories, prayers, and rituals planned by the students and celebrated with the boy's parents. This young hero reminded Monte Cassino School and the city of Tulsa that death is a part of life—a portal into Eternal Happiness with God. (M. Buthod, personal communication, January, 1997)

School Recognition and Awards (What is rewarded?)

Given the special identity and philosophy of Catholic schools, the reward and recognition scheme must emphasize Gospel values and religious mission. Catholic educational leaders need to ask two difficult questions: Does the school reward what it claims to value? Do these awards reflect Gospel values and religious mission?

At Mount Carmel Academy (New Orleans, LA), the principal includes awards that recognize and celebrate Christian witness, for example, service as Eucharistic ministers and as "Come Lord Jesus" prayer leaders. Students who exceed the number of hours required for volunteer service and Christian Life Community members who serve above the call of duty by serving those in need also receive awards.

Some schools espouse important values but reward less important ones. For instance, some schools stress academics but, in reality, revere the cult of the athlete. Similarly, some schools emphasize service, yet do not reflect this ideal in the awards given at graduation. Such inconsistencies lead to cultural confusion.

To align athletic awards more closely with religious mission, Catholic educational leaders might accentuate the virtue of sportsmanship and connect it with Gospel values by creating awards that reinforce and celebrate sportsmanlike behavior. Salesian High School (Los Angeles, CA), reconciled its reward mechanism with a sacred core value, thereby resolving an inconsistency. Because Salesian High School places a premium on service, the school changed the purpose of the Letterman Society and its selection criteria to give appropriate emphasis to peer ministry and service rather than to varsity athletics.

Because graduation is the premier public event where everything a school values is displayed and celebrated, some of the clearest indicators of what a school holds sacred are the awards bestowed at graduation. Among other awards, most schools give a top award to the student or students who embody the school's ideals.

Mount Carmel Academy (New Orleans, LA) integrates Gospel values and religious mission into its graduation recognition and reward scheme. Each year the "Carmel Award" is bestowed upon the graduate who represents the ideals of Carmelite spirituality. Another award, the "Sister Mary Grace Danos Award," is given in memory of the second principal of Mount Carmel Academy. For 25 years, Sister Mary Grace

Consider how your school recognizes and celebrates Christian witness. Check which of the following your school honors:

____ *Eucharistic ministers*
____ *Confirmation candidates*
____ *Christian service work*
____ *Retreat/Prayer leaders*

Other(s):

____ _____
____ _____
____ _____

In light of the check marks, cite what you will do to honor Christian witness:

1. _____
2. _____
3. _____

was a tireless worker, unbelievable fund-raiser with a Midas touch, and aflame with love of God. Each recipient has exhibited these qualities by serving others, supporting worthy causes, and being aflame with love for God.

two notes of caution...

After considering the importance of heroes and heroines—the human symbols of culture—two notes of caution are appropriate. First, schools should avoid "hero worship." Because human nature is flawed, it would be better to emphasize heroic *deeds* not heroic *people*. In schools, populated by young people who are easily disillusioned, hero worship can prove devastating. In terms of what the school rewards, then, *what* is rewarded is critical, not *who* is rewarded.

The second note of caution centers on educators. Can a school honor any one educator too much, especially by associating a school's identity with one or more long-serving teachers or administrators? Honoring any individual's contribution too much can prove especially dangerous when the school's identity hinges upon these individuals which, in turn, confers upon these individuals an inordinate amount of informal power. In a Catholic school, no person should wield this amount of power, holding the school community hostage to the cult of personality.

Catholic educational leaders should also resist the temptation to honor staff members whose lives revolve around the school. Although these individuals may be very well-intentioned, their selfless and tireless service may reflect something that should not be honored, namely, "workaholism." Promoting these individuals as role models endorses one-dimensional, compulsive, and unhealthy behavior. Sacrifice and hard work are laudable but workaholism is not.

Chapter Summary

Heroes and heroines personify a group's shared values, putting a human face on core values. These role models are easy for people to relate to and identify with, and they provide standards that people can strive for. Heroes and heroines may vary with the times, as they are determined at any moment in history by what is valued and who does the valuing.

Youth need role models. In school, who is honored and what is rewarded provide for youth telltale signs of what the school really values. Therefore, it is imperative—for Catholic educational leaders— as architects of Catholic culture—to honor heroes and heroines who exemplify Gospel values and the school's religious mission.

Identify three of your school's top annual awards:

1. _____
2. _____
3. _____

Identify how each of these awards reflects Gospel values and/or your school's religious mission:

1. _____
2. _____
3. _____

Suggest how you might revise these awards in light of your school's religious mission or identify a new award that you might create:

_____
_____
_____
_____
_____
_____
_____
_____

Chapter 5

• Symbols...

Symbols are "the outward manifestation of those things we cannot comprehend on a rational level. They are expressions of shared sentiments and sacred commitment" (Deal & Peterson, 1999, p. 60). Carlyle indicates the importance of symbols, writing, "It is in and through symbols that man, consciously or unconsciously, lives, works and has his meaning" (quoted in Sergiovanni, 1984, p. 4). Symbols oftentimes elicit a powerful emotional response and also exert a mystical power. This may be due to the fact that symbols release feelings of identity and belonging which are basic human needs (Maslow, 1970).

Catholic culture...

Most religions incorporate symbols into rituals and ceremonies, but the Catholic imagination seems to require more than most (Greeley, 1995). Four sacraments use oil, symbolizing preservation of life and the presence of the Holy Spirit. The ritual for Ash Wednesday incorporates ashes to symbolize mortality. Incense symbolizes prayers rising to God. For Catholics, the celebration of the Eucharist centers on the need for nourishment through bread and wine transubstantiated into the body and blood of Christ. For centuries, the crucifix has been associated with the Catholic Church as have rosaries and statues.

school culture...

Objects representing a school and its values are "silent messengers" of culture (Chambers, 1998, p. 35). Mascots, logos, emblems, sports team jackets, class rings, and school colors symbolize a school's identity. Other symbols communicate accomplishment, including the graduation cap and gown, varsity letters, honor society pins and, ultimately, the diploma. Something as simple as the design of school stationery and even the grade of paper can convey tradition, innovation, community, strength, or sloppiness.

Years after commencement, graduates often show a strong sentimental attachment to symbols associated with their *Alma Mater*. School architecture and campus landmarks have strong, compelling associative power. Professional prints of a front entrance, campus gates, school facade, bell/clock tower, school sign, or shrine are popular to loyal alumni and others who feel a strong bond with the school. These visual representations conjure up fond memories of bygone experiences.

Catholic school culture...

In light of the theory that Catholics encounter God and experience faith through analogy, metaphor, and through the five senses (Greeley, 1990, 2000; McBrien, 1994; Tracy, 1981), it follows that Catholic imagination is fed through symbols and rituals. Catholic educational leaders need to be mindful, then, of providing a rich array of symbols and rituals that identify, promote, and celebrate the school's core values and religious mission.

CULTURAL BUILDING PLAN:
CREATE AND DISPLAY A SYMBOL SYSTEM
REFLECTING GOSPEL VALUES AND RELIGIOUS MISSION

Cutler's (1989) observation that schools are "cathedrals of culture" proves instructive for Catholic educational leaders. It is imperative that the symbol system enables people who come into the Catholic school to make a direct connection between the school and its religious identity.

Incorporate religious identity into symbol system

Most schools possess a set of symbols that identify what the school is about. Common symbols are pictures, statuary, emblems, mascots, colors, signs, and clothing.

The school crest captures the essence of Our Lady of Mercy School (Daly City, CA). Designed to incorporate the school's inspiration and history, the school's Dominican heritage is represented by the Dominican Cross with its *fleur-de-lis* points symbolizing those who seek Mary's patronage and a rosary denoting the Dominicans' devotion to the Rosary. The central figure of the crest is Mary, Our Lady of Mercy, surrounded by five stars, each symbolizing one aspect of the educational program at this "Five Star School," that is, a spiritual foundation, academic excellence, fitness for life, personal enrichment, and special services. The crest also incorporates the founding date of the school to indicate its 40+ year history.

The lobby at Aquinas Middle-High School (David City, NE) boasts two symbols capturing the school's essence. One is the school's emblem, artistically incorporated into the terrazzo floor. Within the emblem's lines are symbols representing the life of St. Thomas Aquinas as these relate to the school's work and mission. The open book symbolizes his scholarship. The crown of thorns symbolizes St. Thomas Aquinas' attribution of his scholarship to meditation on the crucified Christ. The chalice symbolizes his devotion to the Eucharist. And, the lighted torch symbolizes the school's mission, namely, to bring St. Thomas Aquinas' love of truth, meditation on the crucified Christ, and devotion to the Eucharist to the students.

Two emblems signify the identity of Mount Carmel Academy (New Orleans, LA) and the person educated there. The first emblem is the seal of the Carmelite Order, the "Escutcheon." The second is the school motto, "With Zeal Am I Zealous with the Lord God of Hosts," taken from the prophet Elijah and describing the student's character. A booklet and formal explanation describing the Escutcheon and the school motto is given to all ninth graders and repeated when students receive their class rings. The school motto is emblazoned on book bags, book covers, stationery, sweatshirts, and handbooks to remind everyone about the school's purpose.

A school's mascot and colors also serve to identify and represent a school's distinctive heritage and culture.

At Skutt Catholic High School (Omaha, NE), the fictitious Sky-Hawk serves as the school's mascot. Symbolically, the SkyHawk soars higher than others of its species, calling others to reach their highest potential and be closer to God. The SkyHawk exhibits the wisdom of learning, self-discipline, and concern for others. Humility and justice guide the SkyHawk in action. Its decisions reflect the prudent use of intellect, will, and emotion for the benefit of others. In addition, the SkyHawk's peers view it as a leader and protector and, though a non-predator, as a fierce but honorable competitor. An opponent knows that the SkyHawk will not quit, that it wins graciously, and accepts loss with dignity. In addition, the SkyHawk loves the beauty and abundant natural resources of its habitat. Its dominant color, green, symbolizes the hope that all creatures will be good stewards of the abundant gifts that God has given humanity. The color black, the presence of all colors, signifies that the SkyHawk embraces diversity and strives toward global unity and respect for the dignity of human life. Its third color, silver, symbolizes the shining light of the salvation promised by God to humanity.

The incorporation of multicultural images into a Catholic school's symbol system reflects the rich cultural diversity cherished by the Church.

At San Xavier Mission School (Tucson, AZ), the school emblem embodies a cross with the maze of the tohono O'odham tribe in a circle. Inside, one finds Native American symbols, including feathers around the sketch of the school building with a cross as the focal point.

For St. Mary's Mission School (Red Lake, MN), in addition to traditional Catholic symbols, significant Ojibwe symbols and paintings are found in the hallways and classrooms and offices. The Thunderbird, an important Ojibwe symbol, is the school's logo. The cross is found within the Thunderbird, symbolizing the integration of the Ojibwe and Catholic belief in the Creator. The eight-pointed star visualizes the Ojibwe belief in God's presence in one's interactions with the Creator, others, and creation.

And, at Nativity School (Cincinnati, OH), because "Jesus is for all people of all cultures throughout all of history," high-quality religious art representing various cultures and historical periods adorns Nativity School. Most are original works, some commissioned for the school. The school boasts a collection of Madonnas reflecting African, Hispanic, European, and contemporary American cultures. Each year, the school displays its collection of Nativity sets from around the world, including sets from Finland, El Salvador, Mexico, Australia, Ireland,

School symbols are "silent messengers" of culture insofar as they convey what a culture values.

Examine your school's emblem or logo.
- *What elements send a religious message?*
- *What elements send a Catholic message?*
- *Can the members of your school community articulate the religious significance of your school's emblem or logo?*

Cite three ways you can educate the members of your school community about the religious symbolism of the school's emblem or logo:

1. _____
2. _____
3. _____

Discuss how you might enhance the religious significance of your school's symbol system (e.g., emblem, logo, mascot, newspaper or yearbook name, school colors, class rings, stationery, etc.):

_____
_____
_____

Italy, Kenya, Peru, Guatemala, France and Australia. Several Nativity sets are gifts from schools with whom Nativity School has exchanged students. Nativity School also honors the memory of Dorothy Day, Stephen Biko, Martin Luther King, Jr., and Archbishop Romero by displaying their pictures and telling their stories in religion class.

At Christ the King School (Daphne, AL), everyone who approaches the school sees a median in the center of the schoolyard. The median contains a green circle with a tree and flowers in the center representing God the Father, three crosses representing God the Son, and a fountain representing God the Holy Spirit. At the end of the median is a statue of Mary. These religious signs inspire both students and parents. Families adopt sections, tending to the flowers and shrubs and making repairs.

Display school and religious symbol system

Many Catholic schools display school symbols and religious images throughout the building and around campus. Some symbols and religious images—the "silent messengers" of the school's core religious values—include the mission statement, crucifix, statues, pictures, posters, and banners. Display areas range from school uniforms to designated bulletin boards to the school foyer to the campus green. Unless an individual is new to a school, its symbol system is oftentimes taken for granted. Therefore, it is important for Catholic educational leaders to ensure that the symbolic meaning associated with the school's symbol system is kept alive through continuous education and promotional efforts.

As people enter Christ the King School (Daphne, AL), they first see its mission statement, the NCEA logo "This is a Christ-centered Zone," and a picture of Pope John Paul II with his arms outstretched. Walking towards the gym people pass by a garden with a statue of Christ which the students have adopted and named "Christ's Garden." They weed it, water the flowers, and trim the shrubs. Every classroom and office displays the school's mission statement, the NCEA logo, a Bible, a statue of Mary, and a crucifix. "My final dream is to build a grotto of the Holy Family," the principal notes. "When this becomes reality, Christ the King will have many symbols to help us think of the divine in the midst of a secular society" (M. Nolan, personal communication, January, 1997).

Mater Dei High School (Breese, IL) promotes the symbol of the Madonna and Child. Beyond printing the symbol on school stationery, programs, and promotional materials, the words from the hymn "Hail Mary, Gentle Woman" appear on banners hanging from the lampposts on the streets outside the school. The banners have the school's Madonna and Child symbol on top and the phrases "Teach us wisdom, teach us love" emblazoned across the bottom. "The banners proclaim to everyone approaching the school what we are about" (J.

Darr, personal communication, January, 1997).

St. Michael School (Greenville, PA) displays statues and pictures of St. Joseph, St. Theresa, St. Michael the Archangel, and Pope Pius X as well as pictures of the Bishop and priests who have served the school and parish. To motivate students and faculty, religious posters adorn the corridors. NCEA banners hang on fences facing Main Street in front of the school's two buildings. Every classroom also contains a crucifix, a statue of the Blessed Mother, and a religious-theme bulletin board.

At St. Mary's School (Edwardsville, IL), each classroom has a prayer board. The classroom teachers and students accumulate names of persons whom the students remember in their classroom prayers as well as at home as they say their morning/night prayers. According to the principal, "Word of this activity has gotten into the community. We get calls from non-parish as well as non-Catholic persons asking for a name to be added to the prayer boards. This project has become a sign of the power of prayer to the community" (J. Johnson, personal communication, January, 1997).

The uniform sweater at St. Cecilia School (Omaha, NE) is emblazoned with the shield of the Sinsinawa Dominican Sisters. The principal explains: "They founded the school in 1907 and have taught here ever since. At one time we had 44. Our traditions and many of our current practices are what they taught us. The principal and several of the teachers are products of the Dominicans right here. We owe them that tribute!" (B. Pryor, personal communication, January, 1997).

Sometimes, stored religious treasures can be refurbished as a tribute and celebration of a school's religious heritage.

At St. Lawrence School (Muncie, IN), the former convent now houses a homeless shelter and because of the alleged conflict between church and state, the stained glass windows had to be removed. The principal notes, "When I became administrator, I found seven windows stacked in a storage room wrapped in foam core. I hired an appraiser and architect and started the plans to install the windows into our school chapel. The parish was excited that we wanted the windows and supported us financially. Many donations were made in honor of deceased parishioners" (M. Arter, personal communication, January, 1997). During the Christmas holidays, builders installed the windows in the school chapel and, during Catholic Schools Week, the parish was invited to an open house. Then, as part of the Bishop's annual visit, he dedicated the windows.

The principal of St. Cecilia School (Omaha, NE) had 40 oak-framed paintings refinished. Originally brought from Rome and hung in the convent when the school was built in 1954, the paintings—including depictions of the Madonna and other religious details from the masterpieces of Fra Angelico, Sassoferrato, Simone Martini, Filipino

Schools are "cathedrals of culture" insofar as they stand as monuments that display cultural values.

Scan your building and campus for evidence of your school's Catholic identity. Check the evidence of your school's Catholic character:

_____ *school campus and grounds*
_____ *school sign*
_____ *school façade*
_____ *entranceway/foyer*
_____ *hallways*
_____ *offices*
_____ *classrooms*
_____ *athletic facilities*
_____ *auditorium*
_____ *student commons/cafeteria*
_____ *school stationery, newsletter, and promotional materials*
_____ *school diploma and other documents*
_____ *school uniform*

Review your check marks. Suggest three plans to enhance the presence of school and religious symbolism in your school and around its campus:

1. _____
2. _____
3. _____

Identify three steps you might take to incorporate or display multicultural Catholic symbolism in your school:

1. _____
2. _____
3. _____

Lippi, Bellini, and Boticelli—are now prominently displayed. "We did research on the paintings and they now hang in our hall and will be part of our discipline-based Art in Religion course….It is a treasure that thrills all of us" (B. Pryor, personal communication, January, 1997).

Some Catholic schools display symbols associated with seasons of the liturgical calendar (Figure 10).

Figure 10
The liturgical calendar

***Spalding Catholic High School (Granville, IA)
and St. Mary's High School (Remsen, IA):***

These schools teach the liturgical calendar by focusing on one symbol and theme during each liturgical season.

Season: Symbol:

Advent   wreaths in each classroom
Theme: *"Let compassion be born anew in our lives"*

Lent   antique tiller in black soil
Theme: *"Let courage turn over the soil of our lives"*

Easter   flowing water and waterfall
Theme: *"Let the living waters of hope flow within you"*

At one school, the graduating class chooses a theme and an accompanying symbol to represent them throughout eighth grade. The principal of Blessed Sacrament School (Alexandria, VA) submits: "Each year our eighth graders are invited to select a Gospel-based theme for their final year at Blessed Sacrament. We then integrate this theme to all aspects of our faith community. One year the eighth graders selected 'God, our fortress and our rock.'"

At the opening school assembly, each student received a small rock and a large rock was placed on a table in the school entrance. Throughout the year we used the rock to relay various messages. At assemblies, we recognized those who were 'rocks' for others. During Advent we placed four candles and evergreens around the rock. At graduation, we invited the graduates to come forward and stand on the rock as a reminder that God is and always will be their rock. At the end of the school year we gave the rock to a teacher who was to receive treatment for breast cancer. As a farewell gift, the graduates gave the school a rock with their graduation year engraved on it. The rock remains in the school foyer, a formidable reminder of 'God, our fortress and our rock'." (M. Dowling, personal communication, June, 1999)

To have a graduating class purchase a religious symbol—of special significance to that class and the school—as its gift is a telltale sign that the school's religious mission has special meaning. The principal of Sacred Heart School (West Des Moines, IA) offers this testimony:

> Each year, the graduating class purchases a gift to present to the school. The Class of 1996 selected a special painting—"Christ at Heart's Door"—which shows Jesus standing at a door with no knob, since he needs no door to enter our hearts when we welcome Him. The Bishop spoke about the painting in his homily at their Confirmation that spring and, at the request of the class, this beautiful gift hangs in the school's entryway as a vivid reminder of them. It also challenges us to make the atmosphere of Sacred Heart School what it should be. (A. Westerhaus, personal communication, October, 1999)

Just as religious images incorporated into the school symbol system and displayed around campus signal what the school community values, religious images worn or displayed by persons engaged in the ministry of education are indicative of what they value. The general public has a tendency to think that if a Catholic educator is wearing a prominent religious symbol, he/she must be a priest, brother, or sister.

When I was a lay principal several years ago, I was asked at the annual Halloween Carnival to take tickets at the senior class haunted house. Parents who took their two young children part way through came back and said "Father, we didn't make it through all the way because the kids were too scared. May we have a refund?" After I returned their money, I wondered why they thought I was a priest. Then it dawned on me that it must be the cross I was wearing around my neck. There is a lesson in this story for lay Catholic educational leaders about the power of personal symbols. If the general public expects women and men religious to wear religious symbols, consider the powerful message it sends when a lay person wears a religious symbol. As a symbolic statement of one's personal commitment to Christ, public ministry, and the school's religious core values and mission, perhaps the lay Catholic educational leader should wear a lapel pin or necklace that symbolizes these personal convictions. If Catholic educational leaders are in public ministry, does it not make sense to wear an appropriate symbol that communicates a commitment to public witness?

Symbols need not be inanimate objects. Educators and other members of the school community also function as "living symbols." The principal of Mount Carmel Academy (New Orleans, LA) expresses this notion:

> More than any other symbol, the administrators, faculty and student body are the symbols that identify the school as Catholic. The word "Catholic" means universal, including everyone. There are numerous

Reflecting upon the concept of personal religious symbolism:
- *What religious symbol has personal meaning for you?*
- *What religious symbol do you or might you wear to reflect your personal spirituality or educational ministry?*
- *What religious symbol do you or might you display to reflect your personal spirituality or educational ministry?*

examples of that at Mount Carmel, where love, respect, and concern for one another is so outwardly shown. Students give so freely of their time and money to the poor and needy in their community. The senior class has taken upon itself to befriend a freshman who is seriously ill by constantly sending prayers, cards, flowers, and books not only to support the child but to support her family as well. Clubs adopt families for Christmas and send school supplies and necessities to a school that serves the poorer of the poor. The religious symbols that best show us as Catholic are the people that make up Mount Carmel Academy. (C. A. Campbell, personal communication, January, 1997)

Chapter Summary

Symbols are visual images or people that represent a culture and what its members cherish. In the educational arena, schools—as "cathedrals of culture" (Cutler, 1989)—symbolize what the larger community values and considers the purpose for schooling and provide a source of identity and meaning.

In view of the power of symbols, in general, and the nourishment they provide the Catholic imagination, in particular, it is incumbent upon Catholic educational leaders—as architects of Catholic culture—to create and display a school symbol system that reflects the school's Gospel values and religious mission.

Chapter 6

• Ritual tradition...

Traditions, ceremonies, customs, and rituals provide meaning to human existence. Some authors distinguish between rituals and ceremonies, treating each separately. They classify rituals as everyday occurrences and ceremonies as special events. In the ensuing discussion, the word "ritual" will serve as an umbrella term dichotomized into "routine" rituals and "ceremonial" rituals.

routine rituals

Because human beings tend to be creatures of habit, "routine rituals" refer to common and repetitive occurrences that people take for granted, oftentimes unconsciously. Despite the routine nature of some rituals—tantamount to "the way we do things around here" (Bower, 1966)—routine rituals perform a valuable cultural function. They serve as token reminders of cultural values and reinforce those values through ordinary human behavior, providing "structure and meaning" (Bolman & Deal, 1997, p. 222).

Catholic culture...

For many people of faith, morning and bedtime prayer as well as prayer before a meal is a routine ritual. For Catholics, the Mass can be a routine ritual in the sense that it is normative for Catholics to attend Mass on Sundays. Other routine rituals include praying the rosary and participating in the Stations of the Cross.

school culture...

Teachers commonly follow routines upon arriving at school. Even though students might not admit it, they engage in routines that provide a sense of security and stability.

School routines can reflect core values. For example, schools that value the individuality of students announce student birthdays. Schools that value student responsibility and participation have students read announcements over the intercom. Schools that have a strict uniform code have routine uniform checks and free dress days to reinforce the uniform's importance. Schools that place a premium on community begin each day with a morning assembly. Schools that value patriotism begin the day with a school-wide salute to the flag.

Catholic school culture...

Ritual routines in Catholic schools can speak volumes about Gospel values and religious mission. For example, in a Catholic school, the inspiration and rationale for a morning assembly, as well as its content and procedure, can take on a religious dimension. The goal should not only be to build community but, more so, to build a "faith community."

If routine rituals can serve to remind people of their culture and its values, then it makes sense that a Catholic school would make prayer as routine as taking attendance. For Catholic schools, St. Paul's exhortation to the people of Ephesus, "Pray always" (Ephesians. 6:18), is still sound advice. What better way to focus students upon the culture animating the Catholic school than through communal prayer? What better way is there to remind students of God's presence in their lives than by providing students with a "constant reference to the Gospel and a frequent encounter with Christ" (Congregation for Catholic Education, 1977, #55) through routine rituals of communal prayer? Hopefully, the ritual of praying throughout the school day, connecting daily life and spirituality with ease, will become so routine that graduates will continue to "pray always" long after graduation.

CULTURAL BUILDING PLAN: NURTURE PRAYER AND WORSHIP THROUGH ROUTINE RITUALS

As with any human relationship, one's relationship with God must be nurtured. With so many concerns competing for attention, however, young people do not always connect their daily life with their spiritual life. The LaSallian tradition of beginning prayers with "Let us remind ourselves that we are in the presence of God" exemplifies a routine ritual through which students center themselves upon God through prayer.

Like St. Paul, who pleaded with early Christian communities to pray, so too, Catholic educational leaders must see to it that every member of the school community, especially students, experience prayer as an integral part of school life.

Praying daily as a school community

Every school day begins at St. Michael School (Greenville, PA) with prayer over the PA system introduced by the principal and led by the students. A prayer list is available for students and teachers to list petitions they would like the community to pray for on that day.

An all-school morning assembly begins each day at St. Mary's High School (Rutherford, NJ). The principal calls this morning ritual "a wonderful community building time" (M. Lanni, personal communication, January, 1997). During this 20-minute ritual, the school community experiences prayer in a variety of ways: music, dance, drama, and traditional spoken prayer. The cycle of the Church year is presented with appropriate ceremonies and various cultures are celebrated with native prayers and music. All members of the school community participate at different times. Following the ritual, the community recognizes individual birthdays and group successes.

At St. Patrick School (Missouri Valley, IA), the entire school

Reflect upon your effectiveness at ensuring that prayer is a routine ritual at your school.
- *When do members of your school community observe you leading prayer?*
- *What resources do you provide yourself, other educators in your building, and parents/guardians to increase everyone's competence and comfort with leading prayer?*

Identify three actions will you take to make prayer a prominent routine ritual in your school:

1. _____
2. _____
3. _____

community meets in the main hall each morning and afternoon to pray. During morning prayer, the teachers and students engage in activities including "mini" plays, music, lighting of candles, and offering food for the food pantry. Morning prayer is so popular that many parents attend. Before students leave school each day, the school community gathers again to pray. The principal writes: "We ask that they remember in their prayers that night anyone in our community who needs prayers. Each Friday we send the students home after saying the 'Guardian Angel Prayer,' asking them to look over our students throughout the weekend" (M. Anderson, personal communication, January, 1997).

Students at St. Ignatius School (Mobile, AL) recite a daily pledge to remind them of their responsibilities to others: "I believe that Jesus is present in each of my classmates and in my teachers and, therefore, all my actions will show my respect for Jesus."

Catholic educational leaders should ensure that, at a minimum, each school day begins with prayer.

Classroom prayer

Many Catholic schools begin each class with a prayer, a classroom practice as routine as taking attendance.

Classroom prayer can be as diverse as the classroom community. A prayer can be read by an individual or recited as a group. Some teachers have students stand for prayer; other teachers have students remain seated. As for the prayers, teachers and students can select readings from scripture, traditional prayers like "The Lord's Prayer," and "Hail Mary," religious music, or inspirational religious reading. One Catholic school alumna spoke about a teacher who began each class informally, having students shout "Yeah God!" This alumna added that no matter where she was in the building, she could hear students shout this prayer seven times each day.

At St. Cyril School (Tucson, AZ), teachers use classroom prayer to connect the school with the parish. The principal reports: "Prayer is a very important and an integral part of St. Cyril School. In the classroom, the teachers have a different group of children every hour and they begin each class with a prayer. Each month, the faculty selects a value and a scripture reading that emphasizes the value for use in daily prayer. Each classroom has volunteered to be prayer partners for the parish's catechumens" (J. Sayre, personal communication, January 1997).

It is important for Catholic educational leaders to recognize that if they are going to require teachers to lead prayer, this requires providing teachers and students tools for prayer. Some principals create a teacher's notebook of prayers, including prayers for all occasions, the seasons of the Church year, prayers before exams, prayers for Advent, Lent, and Thanksgiving as well as theme prayers for various occasions.

Prayer is the consummate routine ritual for Catholic schools. Place a check next to each school activity that begins with prayer:

_____ *assemblies*
_____ *classes*
_____ *class meetings*
_____ *club meetings*
_____ *faculty meetings*
_____ *honors convocation*
_____ *open house*
_____ *orientation*
_____ *parent night*
_____ *prom dinner*
_____ *PTA meetings*
_____ *school board meetings*
_____ *sports team huddles*
_____ *sports competitions*
_____ *sports banquet*

other(s):

_____ _____
_____ _____

_____ _____

Review your check marks. Of the items that you did not check, identify three occasions you will now begin with prayer:

1. _____
2. _____
3. _____

Regarding the importance of providing teachers with resources, the principal of St. Cyril School (Tucson, AZ), offers this testimonial:

To help teachers develop prayer time with the children and to guide their own prayer life, I have purchased a book entitled, *Children's Daily Prayer*, for the school year. Teachers use the book at least once a week to establish prayer as a ritual that the class values and for which the class sets aside a special time. Teachers have told me they feel more confident and encouraged in their faith and the prayer time together is becoming a very natural part of their class. This time together has raised the awareness of everyone of their need for prayers and that each of them can offer prayer to help one another. (J. Sayre, personal communication, January, 1997)

The more routine and natural Catholic educators can make classroom prayer, the more Catholic educators build Catholic culture. Placing students at such ease with prayer is perhaps the most wonderful gift that Catholic educators can offer students.

School-specific prayers

Some schools invoke their school patron or another special saint at the close of every prayer.

At LaSalle Academy (Providence, RI), most prayers end with "St. John Baptiste de LaSalle, pray for us." At Cathedral Prep (Erie, PA), prayers commonly end with, "Mary, Queen of Prep, pray for us." Some schools recite a specific prayer having particular meaning for that school. At St. Ignatius College Prep (San Francisco, CA), students recite St. Ignatius' "Prayer for Generosity." This is the first prayer students learn at freshman orientation and it is the last prayer they say at graduation. Similarly, at Mercy High School (Omaha, NE), Venerable Catherine McAuley's "Suscipe" holds special meaning.

At St. Mary's School (Waterbury, CT), the principal leads the school community in prayer each morning by praying the Novena to Saint Theresa. According to the principal, "The power of the Novena to Saint Theresa is known throughout the greater Waterbury area as is evidenced by the demand for our Saint Theresa prayer cards and the number of requests for special intentions. Our students and their families are aware that miracles happen every day from saying this Novena. We ask our student body not only to pray for miracles and expect miracles but also to identify miracles. Saint Mary's has truly witnessed the power of the Novena to the Little Flower over the years" (M. Josephs, personal communication, January, 1997).

For schools not associated with a religious congregation nor with a saint associated with a popular prayer, Catholic educational leaders should engage the school community in identifying a school-specific prayer (Figure 11, p. 51).

Figure 11
Creating a school prayer

Junípero Serra High School (San Mateo, CA):

Named in honor of Padre Junípero Serra, the Apostle of the Californias (Baja and Alta), Junípero Serra High School was established in 1944 as the Catholic high school for boys in San Mateo County, California. From it beginnings, the school has been staffed by diocesan priests and the laity. In the early 1980s, the school's leaders took two years to formulate a prayer that would solidify the school's Catholic ethos and provide a focus for prayer at Junípero Serra High School. The school's motto, *Etiamsi in via moriar, non revertar* ("Even if I die on the way, I'll never go back"), is based on Junípero Serra's personal motto, *Siempre adelante* ("Always forward") and serves as the foundation for the school's prayer.

The Junípero Serra School Prayer

Lord God, from You comes all that is good, all our talents and abilities. Help us develop these gifts, even when it means hard work. Help us face the reality of working together as a community. When necessary, help us deal with pain and disappointment. Be with us in our endeavors. In the spirit of Junípero Serra, let us never give up. Let this dedication in our lives today help us grow in faith, maturity and life for tomorrow. We ask this through Christ our Lord. Amen.

Blessed Junípero Serra, Apostle of the Californias. Pray for us.

Multi-cultural prayer

In view of the fact that universality and inclusivity are considered core Catholic convictions and that Catholicism is not tied to any single culture, every Catholic school should strive to acquaint students with prayer and worship representing more than one culture. For example, St. Mary's Mission School (Red Lake, MN) incorporates Native American traditions into its prayer life. The weekly prayer circle begins with the cleansing ceremony of smudging with sage ritually enacted by the school secretary who is an enrolled member of the Ojibwe tribe. On special occasions, the liturgies include tobacco offered with the petitions and the proclamation of the faith offered in the four directions.

ceremonial rituals

Ceremonial rituals are special events that display and celebrate core values. Ceremonies mark milestones and possess a "sacred quality" whose effect can be potent (Trice & Beyer, 1993, p. 110), especially when replete with pageantry and drama. For their part, Deal and Peterson note that "without expressive events, any culture will die"

Describe how your school acquaints its students with prayer and worship of various cultures and/or accommodate diverse faith traditions represented therein:

_____

_____

_____

_____

Suggest three additional ways you might ensure that your school community is more inclusive of diverse cultural and faith traditions in its prayer life:

1. _____

2. _____

3. _____

Catholic observances and religious commemorations inspire the Catholic imagination. Check each special religious occasion that your school community celebrates:

_____ *Feast of Our Lady of Guadeloupe*
_____ *Feast of St. Nicholas*
_____ *Christmas Pageant*
_____ *Seder Meal*
_____ *May Crowning*
_____ *Las Posadas*
_____ *All Saints Day*
_____ *Patronal Feast Day*

other(s):

_____ _____
_____ _____
_____ _____

Review your check marks. Identify one or more feasts, holy days, or religious occasions that you do not commemorate at present but plan to in the future:

1. _____
2. _____
3. _____

Cite three actions you will take to enhance the multicultural dimension of your school's religious celebrations and ceremonies:

1. _____
2. _____
3. _____

(1982, p. 63). Furthermore, concerning the importance of ceremony, they assert: "These special events tie past, present, and future together. They intensify one's commitment to the organization and revitalize for challenges that lie ahead" (1999, pp. 94-95).

Catholic culture...

Celebrations and commemorations characterize the Catholic imagination. Ceremonies punctuate the seasons of the Church year. Most notably, the season of Advent culminates with the celebration of Christmas and the season of Lent culminates with the celebration of the Easter Triduum. The annual May Crowning of the Blessed Virgin Mary is another example of a seasonal Catholic ritual.

Just as ceremony punctuates the seasons of the Church year, so too ceremony punctuates significant milestones in a Catholic's life. Through music, processions, costumes, symbols, drama, and pageantry, the celebration of the seven sacraments communicates the significance of human life by linking the individual with the Church community at the deeper level of meaning, purpose, and shared values.

school culture...

School ceremonies are special events that display and celebrate core values. These ceremonies take the form of pep rallies, science fairs, Christmas pageants, ring ceremonies, sports banquets, academic awards convocations, talent shows, and school plays. What is important in terms of building culture is how school ceremonies reflect cherished ideals.

Without doubt, the school's graduation ceremony is the premier public event at which everything the school treasures occupies center stage. Rich in symbolism and pageantry, a well-orchestrated graduation satisfies the human need for drama and builds commitment and loyalty to the institution and its values.

Catholic school culture...

Since ceremonies indicate what is cherished, it is essential for Catholic schools to connect their ceremonies directly to their religious mission. In other words, religious mission should be communicated loud and clear by means of the witness these ceremonies provide. The degree to which their ceremonies are tied to religious culture speaks volumes about what a Catholic school does or does not value.

CULTURAL BUILDING PLAN:
USE CEREMONIAL RITUALS TO SHOWCASE
GOSPEL VALUES AND RELIGIOUS MISSION

It is essential that Catholic schools reflect "Gospel culture" and "faith community" that springs from a sacramental view of life. As architects of culture, Catholic educational leaders should incorporate

Catholic observances and other religious commemorations into the Catholic school "way of life."

Religious Feasts, Holy Days, and Other Commemorative Ceremonies

The Catholic school year should be punctuated with religious ceremonies and observances that mark special occasions and that align with the liturgical year. In addition to popular feast days such as the Feast of St. Nicholas, principals should consider commemorating feast days of saints who hold special significance for their schools.

Catholic educational leaders should not overlook the May Crowning, a traditional Catholic ceremony regaining popularity.

At Villa Maria Academy (Erie, PA), the seniors' final day is called "Mary's Day" and is one of the most revered and anticipated days of the school year. For this day, seniors elect the May Queen, Escort, and members of the May Court.

Not only is Mary's Day a way to honor the patroness of Villa Maria through rituals, Mary's Day honors Mary through loving acts. It is customary on Mary's Day, with students dressed in their best, to send letters of warmth and affirmation to friends, classmates, and teachers. Mary's Day morning begins with a flurry as students deliver their mail to homeroom mailboxes. Next, students attend the Mary's Day all-school assembly.

At the assembly, the senior class bids farewell, presenting a special program. Some seniors share performance pieces. A video highlights the past four years. The assembly concludes with a special song and blessing for the freshmen, sophomores, and juniors along with their leaders. It is an emotional and moving time for the entire student body. Following the assembly, students enjoy a breakfast of homebaked cinnamon rolls and juice, while everyone reads their letters and notes.

The highlight of the day, the May Crowning, follows breakfast. A grotto of flowers adorns Mary's statue on the auditorium stage as the parents and alumni guests fill the auditorium. In the hallways, the entire student body silently forms an honor guard to honor the graduating seniors who process through the darkened halls to the auditorium, silently and reverently carrying lighted candles.

Once all are seated, the members of the May Court—with girls in long white dresses and their escorts in suits and ties—process to the stage for readings from scripture, reflections delivered by the May Queen and Escort, and finally, the crowning ceremony while all sing *Ave Maria*. The ritual concludes as the May Court processes from the auditorium to the gymnasium for a reception.

Multicultural Considerations

Vatican II's emphasis on the cross-cultural nature of the Catho-

The school year is punctuated with special events that mark milestones or achievements. Integrating religious themes reinforces Catholicism's sacramental view of life.

Describe when and how your school connects these events with its religious mission:

_____

_____

_____

Suggest how you might strengthen this connection:

_____

_____

_____

lic Church and the duty of Catholics to work toward cultural harmony (Vatican Council II, 1965d/1996, #42) suggests that Catholic educational leaders should make every effort to increase cultural awareness. To that end, principals should take a multicultural approach to commemorating religious feasts and holy days.

Hispanics now represent 37% of the enrollment at St. Patrick School (Wichita, KS). The principal notes: "Each day the community promotes its diversity as a gift and special opportunity for growth" (D. Wilson, personal communication, January, 1997). The community celebrates at least two Spanish all-school Masses, the Feast of Our Lady of Guadeloupe and *Cinco de Mayo*. To heighten the significance of the Guadeloupe event, Spanish dancers and speakers perform at an assembly. Also, Mariachis provide music at Masses and lunch during the year.

At Christmas time, the St. Cyril School community (Tucson, AZ) celebrates *Las Posadas*. The entire school community walks to three different houses in the neighborhood, knocking on the doors. Lastly, after knocking on the church door, everyone enters a live nativity scene where the classes sing songs in Spanish, and students present readings in Spanish and English. A Mariachi Band then leads the gathering from the church to the courtyard for a fiesta—featuring dancing, the breaking of piñatas, and a meal.

Prayer for wakes and anniversaries of deaths are central in the life of the tohono O'odham tribe, the Native American community served by San Xavier Mission School (Tucson, AZ). At wakes and anniversaries of parents and relatives, the principal invites students to be part of the choir. The songs always include Native American melodies using the drum and rattle. Likewise, when the uncle of a student at St. Cyril School (Tucson, AZ) was murdered, the students in grades 5-8 planned a special liturgy for the family. They also purchased a tree that was planted near the church entrance as a symbol of new life.

True to Catholic tradition of marking life's milestones, students at St. Cyril (Tucson, AZ) commemorate wedding anniversaries. At one school liturgy, the grandparents of two students celebrated their 50th wedding anniversary and renewed their marriage vows. The grandchildren were readers and gift bearers and presented their grandparents with flowers. "This was a wonderful sign of the meaning of commitment for all of the children" (J. Sayre, personal communication, January, 1997).

Emphasizing Religious Mission at Graduation and Other School Events

Ceremonies marking milestones in the school year or the lives of students and faculty provide opportunities for Catholic schools to re-connect with their religious mission. This is done intentionally to nurture in students and the school community, too, the integration of faith and life. For instance, it is common for Catholic schools to usher in each new school year with a "Mass of the Holy Spirit," whereby the school community invokes the Holy Spirit to breathe life into and guide it during the coming school year. In the same vein, some Catholic schools close the school year with a prayer service or Mass of Thanksgiving. Religious themes can also be incorporated into other annual events, like a Ring Ceremony.

At Roncalli High School (Indianapolis, IN), the school community holds prayer services in the fall, winter and spring to commission the student leaders, including captains of the academic teams and athletic teams as well as elected or appointed officers of student organizations. Without a religious emphasis, a school's, secular ceremonies will remain just that—missed opportunities to connect faith and life.

The school community of St. Gabriel School (San Francisco, CA) participates in a cycle of student-planned and student-led liturgies celebrating significant events in the school year. These include: the opening school Mass with installation of Student Council Officers; Mercy Day, a celebration of St. Gabriel's heritage as a school of the Sisters of Mercy; Grandparents' Day with Thanksgiving Liturgy; the Christmas Story Liturgy on the day of dismissal for the Christmas holidays; the Liturgy of the Stations of the Cross during Holy Week; the Graduation Mass for the student body and families of 8th graders; and, the "Moving Up" ceremony on the last day of school when students give thanks for the blessings of the past year and are greeted by the teachers of the next grade as the class moves to its new place in the church.

Like other school communities, students and faculty at The Prout School (Wakefield, RI) celebrate Spirit Week each year. Punctuated with costumes and special events, Spirit Week gives students and teachers the opportunity to pause and celebrate who they are academically, spiritually, athletically, and creatively. Moreover, the enthusiasm and friendly class competition keeps spirits high as the final quarter of the year begins. The Spirit Week theme bespeaks the school's Catholic heritage and religious mission. For example, one year the theme was "community." The question posed during Spirit Week that year was: "What do *I* do to build up the Prout Community?"

Graduation—A Litmus Test for Religious Culture

Graduation is the capstone ceremonial ritual displaying and celebrating school culture.

In many Catholic schools, graduation ceremonies are aligned with their religious mission. Although some Catholic schools incorporate the graduation ceremony within the context of the Mass, the majority of schools sponsor a religious service, the Baccalaureate Mass, and a separate graduation ceremony. If the latter is the case, it is the duty of the Catholic educational leader—as an architect of Catholic culture—to

Identify one school event you would like to reconnect with religious mission:

_____

Cite three actions you will take to accomplish this goal:

1. _____
2. _____
3. _____

ensure that the school's Catholic identity is communicated clearly in the graduation ceremony, which most consider the focal event.

Catholic educational leaders can use different aspects of graduation ceremonies to promote the school's religious identity. Take, for example, the procession. It could include a color guard, including a crossbearer, accompanied by U.S., papal, and state flag bearers. Awards can draw attention to the school's religious mission, especially its values (see Chapter 4).

Perhaps no one can better articulate the school's mission than a graduating senior. At Cathedral Prep (Erie, PA), student speakers are chosen based on their ability to describe the school's mission as their graduating class has experienced it. As Adam Trambley stated in his 1989 baccalaureate address:

> Yes, we do have immense problems. The task for us graduates is not to get mired in old problems, but to find new solutions. And where will we, the future community, business, political, and moral leaders of our city and country, look for solutions…..I think the place we need to look for the answers is in the Good News of Jesus Christ. There, Christ tells us that the meek, the merciful, the single-minded, and the peacemakers shall be blest. There, Jesus tells us to stand up for what is right, whether it means becoming unpopular with the Pharisees or even being crucified. There…we are told to be light for the world and salt for the earth, helping to give the message of Christ to the world and thereby helping to transform it.
>
> We should follow the instructions of Pope John Paul II when he tells us to "Love life, respect life in yourself and in others. Give yourself to the service of life, not the work of death." We must also remember Jesus' commandment to "Love one another as I have loved you." If we can do these things, then the American bishops are correct in their optimism when, in *The Challenge of Peace*, they write, "Let us have the courage to believe in a bright future and in a God who wills it for us—not a perfect world, but a better one. Human hands and hearts and minds can create this better world." (1989, p. 33)

Lastly, the principal could present each graduate with a religious symbol, for example, a Bible, *The Catechism of the Catholic Church*, a statue or picture of Christ or the school's namesake or patron, or another religious symbol or landmark associated with the school. Likewise, the class advisor could read the background profile of each graduate as the diploma is presented, personalizing the ceremony by celebrating the ways each student exemplified the school's religious mission.

Through these and many other expressions, Catholic educational leaders—as architects of Catholic culture—can give prominence to the school's religious identity in the public drama of graduation.

Reflect upon your school's graduation ceremony.
- *How do you showcase/communicate your school's religious purpose at this premier annual event?*
- *How will a guest unfamiliar with your school's religious purpose experience it in the following elements of a typical graduation ceremony:*
  …..Procession?
  …..Awards?
  …..Speeches?
  …..Music?
  …..Gifts to graduates?
  …..Traditions?

Identify three actions that will give prominence to your school's religious purpose during commencement exercises:
1. _____
2. _____
3. _____

Chapter Summary

If routine rituals serve as reminders of cultural values and if Catholic school culture is considered a way of life, then it is imperative for Catholic educational leaders—as architects of Catholic culture—to nurture prayer and worship through routine rituals and make them integral to the school's way of life.

Ceremonial rituals are special episodic events that display and celebrate core values, marking milestones with pageantry and drama. As architects of Catholic culture, Catholic educational leaders should use ceremonial rituals to showcase Gospel values and the school's religious mission.

Chapter 7

• Human communication...

The way human beings communicate is a crucially important building block of culture if only because this is how people share their ideas, values, and what gives them meaning and purpose in life. One of the most efficient and effective ways that human beings share these substantive matters is through language and "storytelling." Good stories inspire and they can also reinforce the ideas and values binding people together in communities that possess meaning and purpose.

language

Ferdinand de Saussure (1857-1913) posited nearly one century ago that language is larger than human speech in the sense that language constitutes any sign system that facilitates communication and understanding (Davis & Schleifer, 1994). In recent decades, theorists have utilized these insights in their studies of organizational culture (Deal & Kennedy, 1982; Deal and Peterson, 1990; Bolman & Deal, 1991; Schein, 1992; Trice & Beyer, 1993).

The link between language and organizational culture cannot be overstated. For one thing, language can increase understanding and communication within groups. Language can also shape attitudes as people use metaphors, slogans/mottoes, jargon, songs/anthems, and gestures to focus attention upon organizational values.

Catholic culture...

Catholicism is replete with language that defines its culture. Vatican II, for example, provided a language system describing the Church in relationship to the world. Defining the Church as the "People of God" (Vatican Council II, 1965c/1966), this language renewed the early Christian notion of vocation and especially the vocation of the laity, namely, to proclaim the Good News of salvation through one's witness in the world (Vatican Council II, 1965b/1996, #2). Likewise, jargon like "Mass" and "parish" and titles like "Father" and "Your Holiness" are uniquely Catholic. Interestingly, tests of religious literacy indicate that Catholics have difficulty defining some of their own jargon, including the terms "paschal mystery," "infallibility," and "Immaculate Conception" (Cook, 1991, p. 86).

Especially in the United States, language is an emotionally charged topic. Within the Catholic community, much of this debate centers on the use of inclusive language, especially in the lectionary. The revised lectionary features more inclusive language. In addition, the language used in songs and anthems has influenced Catholic liturgical and devotional life.

Nonverbal language also pervades Catholic culture. Catholics use the Sign of the Cross to signal prayer. Similarly, Catholics kneel and genuflect in church as a sign of respect for the Blessed Sacrament.

school culture...

Education has its share of terms that are fully understood only by those involved in the field. Among others, these terms include: learning style, authentic assessment, magnet school, active learning, and at-risk student. Sometimes educational terms are abbreviated. People need only say the acronym—LD (learning disabled) or ADD (attention deficit disorder)—to be fully understood by others "in the know." Metaphors like "factory," "baby-sitter," "shopping mall," and "family" have been used for generations to describe the school (Ryan & Cooper, 1995).

Sergiovanni (1994a,b; 1995a,b) explains that language influences schools because it shapes the way people think and he concludes that the primary metaphor which should be used in reference to schools is "community." Unlike stratified organizations governed by contracts, Sergiovanni contends that communities—which rely on relationships that bring people together in working toward a common goal—are built around personal commitments. In a community, there is more of a sense of "we" rather than "I". Interdependence compels members to further common goals as opposed to self-interest. Sergiovanni states his case this way: "...if gangs substitute for family and neighborhood by providing students with the sense of community that they need, then schools must create substitutes for gangs by providing an alternative sense of community that makes more sense to students" (1994a, xiv).

Nonverbal communication in education is as old as schools. For example, students are taught at an early age that if they want to speak in class, they must raise their hand to be recognized by the teacher. Likewise, almost every teacher has a nonverbal cue that communicates to students that it is time to stop talking and settle down to learning.

Catholic school culture...

At the crossroads where Catholic culture and school culture intersect, Catholic schools represent a unique blend of cultures emerging in a distinctive culture variously described as a "Gospel Culture," "Culture of Faith," "Faith Community," or "Culture of Relationships." The messages Catholic educational leaders communicate and the language they use to communicate those messages should reflect, support, and strengthen that which makes the school distinctively Catholic.

CULTURAL BUILDING PLAN:
USE LANGUAGE TO COMMUNICATE
GOSPEL VALUES AND RELIGIOUS MISSION

In his discussion about how leaders exercise symbolic leadership, Sergiovanni speaks of the importance of language and communication:

...symbolic leaders are able to communicate their sense of vision by words and examples. They use language symbols that are easily understood but that also communicate a sense of excitement, originality, and freshness. These efforts provide opportunities for others in the school to experience this vision and to gain a sense of purpose, feeling that they share in the ownership of the school enterprise. (1995a, p. 89)

Deal and Peterson (1990) compare this role with that of a poet in the sense that "[t]he words and images and sincerity principals use to talk about the school or students convey sentiments as well as ideas" (pp. 25-26).

Catholic educational leaders have a duty to play this role through their use of language. Catholic educational leaders not only can relay messages but initiate messages as well. In this regard, Catholic educational leaders are not only poets, they are also "language brokers" who play a pivotal role in determining the school's specialized language. Their verbal and nonverbal language must draw attention continuously to the school's core values and religious mission, keeping these in front of the school community.

Word Choice (Metaphors and Jargon)

A simple modification of terminology through word choice can sharpen the distinction between the mission of a Catholic school and its public and private counterparts. For instance, using "faith community" instead of "community" as a metaphor for the Catholic school makes its religious mission more explicit. Similarly, referring to "Christian service" instead of "community service" clarifies the inspiration for service in a Catholic school as stemming from a Gospel mandate. In addition, people in Catholic schools use language shortcuts like acronyms that have become jargon. One familiar acronym is JUG ("Justice under God"), an acronym invented by students decades ago to describe Catholic school discipline.

When the Director of the Early Childhood Center at Blessed Sacrament School (Alexandria, VA) interviews candidates, terms like "ministry" and "vocation" rather than "job" are used. One candidate remarked that she had a new and deep appreciation for what the teachers at Blessed Sacrament School do. When invited to join the faculty, the candidate was both humbled and inspired to be asked to be part of something much greater than just a job.

The principal also uses language to identify Blessed Sacrament as a *Catholic* school. "Virtue of the month" is "Christian virtue of the month." "Community service" is "Christian service." "Inappropriate behavior" is "un-Christian behavior." There are no lists of "classroom rules," but "the beatitudes and social teachings of the Catholic Church." "Time out" is "Christian reflection" or "examination of conscience."

List two educational metaphors and/or jargon widely used to describe public schools:

1. _____
2. _____

Modify these two metaphors and/or jargon to sharpen the distinction of your school's religious mission:

1. _____
2. _____

Identify two additional terms or phrases that you can modify for use in your school:

1. _____
2. _____

61

Slogans/Mottoes

Many Catholic schools use slogans and mottoes to connect the school's academic purpose and religious mission, thereby encapsulating what they hold sacred. For example, Archbishop Hannan High School (Meraux, LA) emphasizes its motto, *Caritas Vinculum Perfectionis* (Charity leads to Perfection), as its operative principle. This emphasis challenges students to recognize what should permeate every aspect of their lives.

The motto of St. Christine School (Youngstown, OH) emerged from a contest. "St. Christine School—A Learning Environment...A Family of God" now appears on newsletters, brochures, and school stationery. "Sharing the Love of the Heart of Christ," the motto of St. Rocco School (Johnston, RI), is a concise statement of the school's mission. The motto is displayed prominently throughout the building and in school publications as a constant reminder of the school's religious mission.

Every school in Bay St. Louis (MS) distributes a "My child is an Honor Roll Student at..." bumper sticker and some parents asked why Bay Catholic Elementary didn't distribute one. Eventually, the school community developed and distributed a bumper sticker reflecting its religious mission. It reads: "At Bay Catholic All Students are Honored."

Mercy High School (Omaha, NE) featured the slogan "Faith in the Future" in its multi-year, multi-million dollar capital campaign. The slogan reflects a conscious attempt to connect the capital campaign with the school's religious mission and identity.

Gestures

Reflecting Catholic tradition, prayers in Catholic schools should begin with the Sign of the Cross. The principal of Santa Margarita Catholic High School (Rancho Santa Margarita, CA) describes another gesture incorporated into school culture:

> One of the first school customs students learn at Ninth Grade Orientation is that students at Santa Margarita Catholic High School stand when an adult, especially a guest, enters a room. This school custom springs from the biblical virtues of honor/respect (1 Peter 1:17) and hospitality (1 Peter 4:9; Romans 2:13). As simple as this gesture is, standing as adults and guests enter a room continually reinforces these Gospel values by providing students many opportunities to show respect for elders and hospitality to guests. Visitors who come to our campus tell us how special and surprised they feel when they encounter this school customary gesture. (M. Hemenway, personal communication, June, 1999)

Explain how your school's slogan/motto elucidates its religious mission:

_____

_____

_____

Create a slogan/motto either for your school or for a particular school program or activity that reconnects your school with its religious mission:

_____

_____

_____

_____

Songs/Anthems

One only needs to listen to the school song in the holiday classic, *Bells of St. Mary's*, to recognize the power of an anthem to emote affection for a school, in this case, the much-beloved St. Mary's.

At Archbishop Hannan High School (Meraux, LA), the school leaders and faculty annually review the school's *Alma Mater* with the students to show how the song's words give their lives meaning as a school community. The principal adds: "Our emphasis lies on the importance of the institution of the school (and, by extension, the Church) as a focal point in the formation of a group of believers. The institution as a rallying point, a symbol for those ideals we hold important as Catholics, is carefully examined through the words of the *Alma Mater*." (J. Serio, personal communication, January, 1997)

School Communications

Many Catholic educational leaders intentionally reference Gospel values and the school's religious mission in written and oral communications.

Every other Wednesday, the principal of St. Cyril School (Tucson, AZ) sends home a publication called the *School Express* which includes "Principal News," a segment designed to update parents about various activities, to recognize students, faculty/staff, and parents. Student poetry and other creative writing, parenting information, and articles or information about Church teaching are also included. *School Express* also promotes the "Scripture and Value of the Month," provides a prayer list of members of the community and relatives who are ill, have died, or have special events, and includes a weekly prayer for families.

Some schools are careful to use language that reflects and concretizes religious mission. Believing that principals are leaders of a faith community within a school and must offer support and spiritual sustenance to parents, the principal of All Souls Catholic School (South San Francisco, CA) launched several initiatives to promote a home-school partnership:

- Parent Education Program: Guest speakers are invited different nights during the year to discuss relevant topics which respond to family needs.
- Parenting Newsletter: This publication is sent monthly to the each student's parents/guardians to assist them in the formation of religious values in their children and to assist them in adult faith development. Faith building literature is integrated within parenting articles.
- Parent Resource Lending Library: The lending library, which contains books, videos, and cassette tapes, provides parents with practical ideas that promote student success and more effective parenting.

Assess a recent issue of the school newsletter or a letter you wrote to students, parents, or teachers.

- *What evidence communicates Gospel values and/or your school's religious mission?*

- *How might this document be modified to better communicate Gospel values and/or your school's religious mission?*

63

The principal of Saint Michael School (Greenville, PA) also sends a monthly school newsletter to parents, parishioners, and alumni. The principal notes: "We feature good news about the accomplishments of our alumni and how the message, community, and service ideals are being lived by our students and teachers. We also include short prayers and ideas for celebrating feasts and seasons in the Catholic tradition" (M. Lipani, personal communication, January 1997).

The letter in Figure 12 illustrates how a Catholic educational leader can connect Gospel values with the school's religious mission. The italicized portions of the letter indicate modifications to a standard form letter.

Figure 12.
Modifying school letters to incorporate the school's religion mission

April 15, 2000

Miguel Lopez
1313 Cathedral Lane
Anytown, USA

Dear Miguel,

I want to personally congratulate you for being accepted into the International Baccalaureate Diploma Program. Your selection by the faculty committee is affirmation of your exemplary work habits and your positive attitude toward learning.

The Letter of James (1:17) states: "Every good gift and every perfect gift is from above, and comes down from the Father of lights...." I want to commend you for developing your God-given talents of the mind to their fullest.

I wish you much success in the IB Program and I hope you find it both challenging and rewarding. May IB benefit you the way it has many of our past graduates.

Good Luck!

Sincerely yours in Christ,

Dr. Maureen McCarthy, Principal
St. Mary's High School

---

stories

Stories are touchstones of culture captured in human experience, communicating messages and teaching lessons. The beauty of stories is that they provide an entertaining and colorful form of instruction which appeals to both mind and emotion and to young and old alike (Gardner, 1995), all of which makes the story easier to remember. The importance of stories and storytelling—for communicating and developing organizational culture—cannot and should not be underestimated by an organization's leaders (Bolman & Deal, 1997).

Catholic culture...

The central story of all of Christianity is the birth, death and resurrection of Jesus. Catholics, however, entertain many more story forms to reinforce the central Paschal Mystery. For instance, legends are part and parcel of the Catholic experience. Marian apparitions like those at Lourdes, Fatima, and Medjougorie appeal to the Catholic imagination because they involve supernatural events like miraculous cures, etc.

Sociologist Andrew Greeley (1995) opines that stories appeal to the Catholic imagination and are foundational for how Catholics experience religion. As Greeley argues, "Religion is experience, image and story before it is anything else and after it is anything else. Simply put, 'Catholics like their heritage because it has great stories' " (p. 32).

school culture...

Stories abound in schools because stories provide a medium to illustrate core values in a relevant, personal, and concrete fashion. "Stories ground complicated ideas in concrete terms, personifying them in flesh and blood. Stories carry values and connect abstract ideas with sentiment, emotion, and events" (Deal & Peterson, 1990, p. 26).

Stories can also persuade. Johnston (1987) tells of a conversation he witnessed between two faculty members. The younger of the two was complaining about how the union straightjacketed faculty independence and initiative. The older colleague responded by telling stories about the administrative fiefdoms prior to the union. From then on, the younger faculty member looked at the union differently. Stories are credible because they are about real people. Persuasive stories are more effective than mountains of evidence in convincing people of a point of view.

Some stories become institutional "sagas" relating pivotal events. These accounts might center on the school's founding, other watershed moments, or the ways people responded to those events. Many sagas are carried through the school's informal communications network by members of the community who "remember when…" (Johnston, 1995).

Catholic school culture...

Situated at the intersection of Catholic culture and school culture, Catholic school communities possess unique stories. One such story resounds through Elk County Christian High School (St. Marys, PA). As the principal relates this story:

The 1994 Keystone Cross Country Invitational provides an excellent story that draws attention to a significant part of the religious mission of Elk County Christian. Respect and appreciation for individual differences is a central theme in the school's religious mission. Jesus embraced marginalized persons to help Him build the faith community around forgiveness and love. His ministry was directed in large part to those whom society shunned: people with disabilities (Luke 7: 18-23), children (Matthew 18:1-6), and the poor (Matthew 5:12).

This particular Saturday morning, the principal engaged the Junior High in a team prayer: "Thank you, Lord, for giving me the ability to run. With your help, I will do my best. Win or lose, I will run in the name of your son, Jesus Christ." I also encouraged the Junior High team to keep close watch on the Varsity team as theirs was an example of hard work, dedication, and camaraderie that typically lends itself to team success. As it turns out, the Junior High squad delivered a lesson of their own in this rugged 1.9 mile race through woods, over roots, and on winding pathways.

It so happened that the Junior High girl's team had, among others, a bonafide running star, Jessica, and also a young lady with cerebral palsy, Elaine. These teammates were truly at the opposite ends of the spectrum. After only one-half mile of running, Jessica took her usual place at the front of the pack of the one-hundred plus participants and Elaine settled in some 50 yards behind the entire group. Both wore the strains of racing on their face ... two young "bookends" moving steadily toward the same finish line. One gliding in a seemingly effortless fashion, the other showing a laborious effort with each stride. When the race concluded, true to form, Jessica established a new course record and finished to an ovation. Some ten minutes later, Elaine limped her way to the very same home stretch to a thunderous applause. Elaine responded with her own special version of a "sprint" finish as her teammates, her competitors, and the spectators wiped their eyes filled with tears. The irony of this first Lady Crusader and last Lady Crusader achieving the victory of finishing was truly symbolic of the school's mission and values as a faith-filled community.

The Varsity? They ran very well; in fact, the team earned top honors in its division. However, the lesson of the day was delivered by the Junior High girls. On this day, the "marginalized" built the faith community and earned a medal of respect and dignity for those who achieve by way of their own uniqueness.

This is the religious message students at Elk County Christian High School hear time and again: while all have the same Heavenly goal in mind, as a result of one's unique and God-given abilities and talents, all undertake different paths to this same end. (J. Wortman, personal communication, January, 1997)

The stories that resound throughout Catholic schools should spring from the central story of Christianity—the life, death, and resurrection of Jesus Christ—and the ensuing story of the Church as a "People of God." Additionally, Catholic school communities should cultivate local stories—myths, legends, and sagas—about their members and watershed events, both past and present, that reinforce the religious core values upon whose foundation these schools are built and continue to prosper.

CULTURAL BUILDING PLAN:
TELL STORIES THAT COMMUNICATE
GOSPEL VALUES AND RELIGIOUS MISSION

Although storytelling is not typical fare in a principal's certification program, because of this important leadership role, the principal should function as the school's chief storyteller who conveys what is important and provides instruction about core values. If the principal believes innovation is important, it would be important that the principal tell stories about innovation. If community is a value, then the principal should spin tales about community (Gardner, 1995).

Deal and Peterson (1999, pp. 55-56) use Hank Cotton of Cherry Creek High School as an example of a principal who told stories to reinforce school core values. Cotton developed a bank of stories he could draw upon to convey his message. His dozen or so stories included themes like success through struggle, the merits of working together, and innovation. On a related note, Johnston (1987) suggests that instead of relating school success in terms of test scores or statistics, it might be more captivating and meaningful to the community if these facts are related through "people stories." Some schools set aside a portion of each faculty meeting to tell success stories that illustrate and reinforce school values.

Envisioning how stories can strengthen school culture, Catholic educational leaders might consider developing a bank of stories that convey what is sacred in the school and illustrate something unique about the school's religious mission. These stories might answer such questions like: Where have we been? Where are we going? Who are we? Who do we want to become? This bank of stories might incorporate school heroes, founders, legendary teachers, and students past and present, all of whom embody the school's ideals and turning points in its history. Regardless of the type of story, each needs to be inspiring.

Identify one of your school's core religious values or charisms:

_____

Sketch a school myth or actual event that bespeaks this value or charism:

_____
_____
_____

Discuss how you might lead the faculty to begin each meeting by sharing stories that reflect your school's religious values and charisms:

_____
_____
_____
_____

Because inspiring stories can speak to the core values and religious mission of Catholic schools, Catholic educational leaders would do well to build Catholic culture through storytelling rather than through policies, mandates, and memos. For example, at Mercyhurst Prep (Erie, PA), one such story focuses upon the determination of the school's founding religious congregation. As Sister Bertha Michalik, RSM, regales whenever she tells this story, the Sisters moved into the building at the beginning of the school year in 1963 even though construction had not been completed. The Sisters believed the workers were not working fast enough and so, to speed up construction, the Sisters moved the students into the building even though there was neither heat nor electricity. During those first few weeks, the teachers and students had to congregate near the windows for light. And, before the cafeteria was completed, everyone heated their lunch with Bunsen burners. This story continues to inspire this heritage of determination and pioneering spirit that identifies Mercyhurst Prep.

Likewise, one of the most cherished traditions at Duchesne Academy (Omaha, NE) and other Sacred Heart Schools the world over, is the devotion to and veneration of *Mater Admirabilis*. This fresco is found at the *Trinita Dei Monti*, a convent of the Society of the Sacred Heart, not far from the famous Spanish Stairs in Rome. The fresco was painted by a young novice, Pauline Perdrau, who asked if she could paint a fresco of Our Lady. Pauline was very disciplined when it came to painting and would paint 7 or 8 hours at a time. When she painted *Mater's* face, she spent 13 hours painting without stopping. Pauline completed the painting on July 1, 1844, but the paint was not dry. Because of this, the colors seemed to glare and did not meet with the approval of Reverend Mother de Coriolis. She demanded that the painting be erased but was persuaded to wait until after the painting dried, demanding that the painting be covered until then. When the day came, the work that Reverend Mother saw moved her to tears because of its beauty.

During a visit in 1846 to *Trinita Dei Monti*, Pope Pius IX was so taken by the fresco's beauty that he exclaimed, "She is most admirable!" Shortly after this experience, Pius IX blessed the painting, conferring the title of "*Mater Admirabilis*," and made October 20th the feast in her honor. Now, *Mater Admirabilis* is the patroness of studies at every Sacred Heart school and, because of her patronage, this image is displayed prominently at every Sacred Heart school.

At Duchesne Academy, sophomores study the story of *Mater Admirabilis* and Mary's other titles as well as her life, devotion, and special qualities. After completing this study, each student is presented a *Mater* medal by a woman chosen by the student because she emulates *Mater's* special qualities. This ceremony, celebrated at a special Mass,

Suggest three actions you will take to encourage the use of oral or written storytelling that conveys your school's religious values or charisms:

1. _____
2. _____
3. _____

Discuss what you might do to preserve your school's legends, myths, and sagas to prevent them from being lost or forgotten:

_____
_____
_____
_____

occurs at every Sacred Heart school. This is a particularly joyous celebration for the entire Duchesne Academy community.

Chapter Summary

Because human communication is a crucial building block of culture, Catholic educational leaders—as architects of Catholic culture—are uniquely positioned to connect the school's language system and communications with Gospel values and religious mission. One way to make this vital connection is through "storytelling." Catholic educational leaders should develop a bank of inspiring stories that remind the school community of it religious heritage and reinforce the Gospel values that continue to be its legacy.

Chapter 8

- **History...**

In the most general sense, history refers to a group's shared past, encompassing past people and events that influence the present. History shapes persons and groups, providing insight into and understanding about who they have been. In addition to its usefulness as a tool to explain and define, another important facet of history is its power to bond people (Bellah, Madsen, Sullivan, Swidler, & Tipton, 1985).

Catholic culture...

Catholicism's distinctive core belief is that God's truth is revealed through Scripture and Tradition. This cumulative wisdom of the past begins with the evangelists and extends through the Christian centuries in the Fathers of the Church like Ignatius of Antioch, Cyril of Alexandria, Gregory of Nyssa, and Augustine of Hippo. This tradition carries through to the present era through its authentic interpretation by the Magisterium.

To understand the movement of the Holy Spirit in the post-Vatican II Church, one must understand how the Church arrived at this moment in history. For centuries, the pivotal events surrounding the Protestant Reformation and the Catholic Counter-Reformation shaped how Catholics viewed themselves in relation to the rest of Christendom. But, a paradigm shift occurred with the Second Vatican Council, the aftershocks of which are still reverberating today.

In *Reshaping Catholicism*, Avery Dulles (1988) delineates 10 themes of Vatican II identifying this paradigm shift in the Church's thinking about itself and the world. His objective in writing this book is to indicate the pivotal importance historical events play in understanding current events and human experience. Dulles makes clear that the full impact of Vatican II is yet to be known and will continue to unfold well into the next century.

In addition to understanding the history of the global/universal Church, American Catholics need also to understand the Catholic experience shaped by their forebears on these shores. It is this shared past that informs the collective identity and imagination of American Catholics as they become the Church of the new millennium.

Where Catholic education is concerned, American Catholics need to understand the "siege mentality" of their forebears in the immigrant church of the 19th century to understand the origins of the Catholic school system in the United States (Buetow, 1985; Dolan, 1985; Walch, 1996). Each generation must answer questions about educating youth and the role Catholic schools will play, if any. As Catholics better understand how their forebears answered questions about educating youth, present and future generations will be better able to make informed decisions.

While Catholics are no longer under siege, there are those who argue that the Church is experiencing a different kind of siege, that of secularism and irreligion. Ironically, Jacobs (1997) notes, the trend of disestablishing religion in the public schools was supported by the Catholic community in the 19th century because of the Protestant bias public schools exhibited in prayer and instruction.

On a related note, as the costs associated with operating Catholic schools have escalated dramatically in recent decades, some would argue that these schools require too much sacrifice to keep them solvent. Yet, a careful reading of history will reveal earlier struggles of equal or greater magnitude involving Catholics who were a poor, oft-discriminated against, immigrant people. A 1987 study using data collected by the Gallup Organization concluded that Catholics have more resources and political and social clout than ever before (Gallup & Castelli, 1987). The struggle today is rooted not in finances but in a crisis of commitment (Greeley, 1985, 1990; Greeley, McCready, & McCourt, 1976).

school culture...

If one wants to understand a school's culture, one must look to its past (Deal, 1985, 1993; Deal & Peterson, 1990, 1999). Delving into a school's history can be instructive because it is there that one will discover the origins and evolution of its core values.

Logic dictates that a school's structure and fundamental beliefs about curriculum, the learning process, discipline, and teacher-student interaction develop over time. Knowing the intentions of the school's founders and other towering figures in its history, as well as the major turning points, can be quite illuminating (Sergiovanni, 1995a).

Attention to school history is important for another reason: history builds community. Awareness of its history enables a school to give students the rootedness and anchoring they desperately need for their personal development. Moreover, a sense of heritage can help students become attached to enduring values and feel a sense of belonging to a community of people preceding and following after them.

It is for no little reason, then, that some of the most respected and sought-after schools boast long-standing traditions and a rich past upon which the present and future are built. This is because people view these schools as strong, stable, and enduring, yet able to change with the times. To outsiders, there is a certain sense of comfort and confidence these perceptions provide. For insiders, there is strength that is gained from memories of past achievements and struggles.

Catholic school culture...

Attention to history and heritage in Catholic school communities flows naturally from a faith tradition. Being a "community of memory" "that does not forget the past" (Bellah *et al.*, 1985, p. 153), should be an essential characteristic of every Catholic school. Besides its own past, each Catholic school community must remember the focal memory of its existence—the life, death, and resurrection of Jesus Christ. Everything about a Catholic school experience must remind students of the person of Jesus Christ, the Risen Lord. As Catholic educational leaders combine school memories with the memory of Jesus Christ, the Risen Lord, Catholic schools become "communities of hope" (Congregation for Catholic Education, 1982 [#26], 1988 [#11,12,13]; Jacobs, 1996 [pp. 58-61]; National Conference of Catholic Bishops, 1972 [#9]).

CULTURAL BUILDING PLAN: REDISCOVER THE SCHOOL'S RELIGIOUS AND HISTORICAL HERITAGE

Passing on the religious heritage of Catholic schools from generation to generation appeared much easier when religious orders operated the schools if only because continuity was more obvious. Attention to heritage was part of the makeup and training of young religious, much of which was passed on through an oral tradition. Today, with lay people of diverse backgrounds and experiences moving in and out of Catholic schools more frequently, this is no longer the case. For Catholic school leaders, attention to heritage must be deliberate and systematic (Jacobs, 1996, pp. i-iv).

Two ways to conceptualize Catholic school heritage would be latitudinally and longitudinally.

Latitudinal heritage refers to making each Catholic school community aware of the common heritage it shares with other Catholic schools. Latitudinal heritage is a corporate heritage in the sense that it recognizes a school as one member in a network of schools. Students share things in common with others who sit in desks in the local community and around the world. Some Catholic educational leaders have created a network based upon a shared heritage, name, or namesake—Seton or St. Patrick, for example.

Longitudinal heritage refers to the history of a Catholic school. Many schools have long and rich histories of which students should be made aware. Each school's history contains people and events shaping the school today. A school's history reveals its origins, why it was built and why it continues, the legacy of shared religious values, and the major players in the school's history.

All Catholic schools have a religious legacy that needs to be transmitted to the next generation. This requires intentionality on the principal's part.

Written History

In an article dealing with pathways to school effectiveness, Deal (1985) underscores the importance of heritage and suggests that "a beginning point is to explore and document a school's history" (p. 615). When a new principal begins service in a school, one of the

Reflect upon the phrases "community of memory" and "community of hope" as each relates to your school. Discuss how these two phrases are related in terms of your school:

Relate an incident in which you heightened your school community's awareness of its latitudinal heritage:

Identify an incident in which you heightened your school community's awareness of its longitudinal heritage:

Read your school's written history. Check which of the following items are included:

_____ *founding/origins*
_____ *historic and heroic figures*
_____ *struggles/successes*
_____ *turning points/mile stones*
_____ *red letter dates*
_____ *core values/charisms*
_____ *traditions*
_____ *school landmarks*
_____ *legends*
_____ *pictures/photographs*

Other:

_____ _____
_____ _____

Suggest two ideas to revise/ update your school's written history:

1. _____
2. _____

Cite two school publications and/or promotional materials that do not include your school's history but should:

1. _____
2. _____

first documents the individual should read is the school's history which provides baseline information about how the school got to where it is now.

Since an historical account is a touchstone to a community's past, it is important to include a brief history in all publications like brochures, handbooks, and yearbooks. This account could be as concise as a timeline or set of "red letter" dates. A lengthier historical narrative with pictures could be a publication in itself. Some schools use the tenure of their principals to organize the school's history. Other approaches include using decades or anniversaries, watershed moments (e.g., a change to coeducation), themes, or groupings of years that dovetail naturally.

Once written, the school's history should be updated periodically. Natural times include: re-accreditation, major school anniversaries, or changes in school leadership. In the last case, updating the school's history with a change in administration should be as second nature as an audit of the school's finances. Both are natural ways to bring closure to a chapter in the school's history. As a cautionary footnote, one problem with waiting for a milestone or anniversary to update the school's history is that it becomes more difficult to reconstruct as years pass and personnel change.

Prominent Displays of Historical Artifacts

Whenever someone enters a school, walks through the halls, and carefully observes what is displayed, the experience should provide a keen sense of what the school community holds sacred. Where a school's heritage is valued, pictures of the graduating classes are displayed chronologically as are portraits of past school leaders. Most schools chronicle their history by displaying athletic trophies; other schools display pictures of the cast of the annual school play. Some schools designate a "wall of time" that chronicles school history, while others designate a permanent exhibit, to display artifacts from the school's history. Some schools allow each graduating class to paint a wall mural commemorating that class's experiences.

Where religious heritage is concerned, a portrait/statue of the school's namesake or patron should be displayed prominently. Some schools display smaller versions in each classroom. It is also important to include items that speak to the school's religious heritage and mission. These might include: class retreat banners, old religion textbooks, programs for special liturgical celebrations, pictures of students participating in service projects, prayer, retreats, and the sacraments.

In 1983, the Carmelite Sisters celebrated their 150th year of ministry in Louisiana. At that time, a celebration was held in the parish where the Sisters first located, a completely different area in the city than the congregation's current location. The lobby of Mount Carmel

Academy (New Orleans, LA) now displays a large mural painted by Sister Baptist depicting places where the Sisters have served as well as the original Mount Carmel Academy.

School Archives and Museum

Catholic educational leaders who have tried to collect/gather artifacts or mementos for class reunions or school anniversaries know how difficult it is to retrieve past yearbooks, newspapers, uniforms, play bills, special event programs, photographs, and diplomas. All too few schools boast a staff member who serves as archivist. This is unfortunate because history is dynamic and must be regularly attended to.

In light of the significance of history, it is important for Catholic educational leaders to designate a staff member to serve as the school archivist. In this capacity, an official archivist might keep a scrapbook of newspaper clippings, collect and catalog school documents as well as posters and programs of school events, and capture school events on film.

Some Catholic school communities have developed small museums where school artifacts are displayed (Figure 13, pg. 80). San Xavier Mission School (Tucson, AZ), for example, is associated with a parish that boasts a parish museum. The history of the school as well as its artifacts are kept there because of the school's association with the historic Church of San Xavier Mission, which celebrated its 200th birthday in 1997. The school is the oldest in the diocese and the first in the State of Arizona, founded in 1864 for the tohono O'odham tribe in the San Xavier District.

Patronal Feast and Founders' Day

Some schools use their school patron's feast as an opportunity to highlight the school's religious heritage. Many schools, especially those with ties to religious communities, annually commemorate the school's founding and founders. Festivities usually include a religious service such as a "Founders' Day Mass." Annual events that commemorate a school's patron and/or founders have a great deal of value considering the ever-changing face of the student body and faculty. At the secondary level, if a school celebrates its heritage each fifth anniversary, the events are held for an entirely new student body each time.

There are many ways to honor a school's namesake, patron, or founders. For example, the feast day of the patroness of Mother Seton Regional High School (Clark, NJ) is commemorated with a school-wide liturgy. At this annual liturgy, students present highlights of Saint Elizabeth Ann Seton's life. One year, for example, a statue and relic of Saint Elizabeth Ann Seton were included among the offertory gifts. Following Mass, the student council president offers a heartfelt thanks to the Sisters of Charity for their mission at the school. Then, the

---

Scan your school building and campus. Check which of the following artifacts are displayed either continuously or periodically:

____ *play bills*
____ *handbooks*
____ *yearbooks*
____ *scrapbooks*
____ *school pennants*
____ *statues*
____ *graduation programs*
____ *curriculum guides*
____ *uniforms*
____ *prom favors*
____ *report cards*
____ *school awards*
____ *school seal/emblem*

Other:

____ _____
____ _____

Propose three actions you will take to showcase your school's historical and religious heritage:

1. _____
2. _____
3. _____

Explore where you might place and/or give greater prominence to a school archives/museum:

_____
_____
_____
_____

Identify who you might designate as the school's archivist/historian:

_____

Figure 13.
A Catholic school museum

Duchesne Academy (Omaha, NE):

The Religious of the Society of the Sacred Heart have given spirituality, tradition, and strong intellectual values to the women who have attended Duchesne College and Academy of the Sacred Heart. Spanning 118 years, this tradition continues in Omaha.

To preserve a record of this heritage, a museum has been established on the Duchesne campus. Many artifacts and photographs record not only Duchesne's history, but also the women who came to Omaha to establish this institution. The museum also depicts many of Duchesne's religious traditions, including May Crowning ceremonies and Masses in honor of *Mater Admirabilis*, St. Madeline Sophie Barat—foundress of the Society in 1800—and St. Rose Philippine Duchesne—frontier missionary who brought the Society of the Sacred Heart to the United States. Other artifacts, such as medals and wreaths awarded at Prize Day, uniforms worn by students at Duchesne, and textbooks are displayed.

This museum serves not only as a learning center for the young women who come to Duchesne Academy, but also as an archive of the achievement of the Society of the Sacred Heart and the young women whom they instructed and nurtured.

Describe how your school annually commemorates its history and religious heritage through its patron's feast and/or founder's(') day:

_____

_____

_____

_____

Identify three ways you might improve this annual commemoration or the steps you will take to commemorate your school's patron saint and/or founder(s):

1. _____
2. _____
3. _____

faculty hosts a hot chocolate breakfast for the entire school community.

St. Maria Goretti High School (Philadelphia, PA) celebrates St. Maria Goretti's birthday in October with a special prayer service. In religion classes, students view *Fourteen Flowers of Pardon*, a video chronicling the saint's life. At graduation, seniors receive a 5 x 7-inch picture of St. Maria Goretti.

When St. Stephen School (San Francisco, CA) opened in 1952, the Bishop invited the Sisters of Mercy to administer and teach at the school. Over the years, the celebration of Mercy has become the school's guiding spirit. Each year the school community celebrates Mercy Day. By telling the story of Venerable Catherine McAuley's love for the poor, the teachers engage students in discussions to help them develop an awareness and concern for the needy and to renew the spirit of the Foundress of the Sisters of Mercy. This yearly renewal includes several Mercy Day events—a children's liturgy, special luncheon for the faculty, and treats for the students.

Other schools have instituted "Foundation Day" to recall and celebrate their founders. At Mercyhurst Prep (Erie, PA), Mercy Foundation Day is celebrated on December 12, the anniversary of the founding of the Sisters of Mercy in Dublin in 1831 by Venerable Catherine McAuley. This celebration recalls the school's foundresses, the Sisters of Mercy of Erie. Foundation Day is an event for the faculty/staff and the Sisters of Mercy, giving the faculty/staff the opportunity to honor and enjoy the company of the Sisters of Mercy, who worked and prayed the school into existence in 1926 and continue to sustain it. On Foundation Day, the faculty/staff and Sisters share a special meal. After the meal, the MPS show choir—a select group of talented singers and dancers—entertain the adults with their holiday show. Several students also present original poems and songs. Lastly, Foundation Day is used to present the Sisters with a Christmas gift.

To emphasize the responsibility each generation bears to keep a school dynamic and its legacy alive, some Catholic school histories describe their founders in terms of past, present, and future. As a way to reconnect a school community with its heritage or as a way to chart a new course, Catholic educational leaders might consider the notion of "refounding" to reconnect the school's founding purpose and charism in light of contemporary needs. For Catholic educational leaders, initiating a refounding process, in addition to, or as part of state/regional reaccredidation or strategic planning, can accentuate the school's religious nature and its Catholic roots.

School Anniversaries

School jubilees provide the perfect opportunity to focus attention on heritage through the pomp and circumstance of pageantry and ceremony. Anniversaries can serve as a rallying point for a school's constituencies—its founding religious community, alumni, teachers, past teachers, parents, past parents, current students, and benefactors—to come together and celebrate the school's mission. In times of rapid change especially, an anniversary can provide an occasion to build a bridge between past, present, and future.

The principal of St. Patrick School (Missouri Valley, IA) reports:

Our school recently celebrated 80 years of Catholic education. We did all of the usual anniversary things, including an anniversary dinner with the Bishop. At the dinner I had one of our students in 6th grade speak about the school and its history. This student's great-grandfather had been the person who started the process of building the school by selling 40 acres of land and donating it to the building fund. Many people commented on how special it was to have this student talk about what this school means to him and his family. It was very moving to hear about their family's sacrifices. It proved to be a wonderful way to connect past with present. Little did the grandparent know that 80 years later, one of his great-grandsons would be in the school. (M. Anderson, personal communication, January, 1997)

Describe when and how your school celebrated its last major anniversary. How did this celebration highlight the school's religious and Catholic heritage?

_____

_____

_____

_____

When is your school's next major anniversary?

_____

Provide three ideas to highlight your school's religious heritage and Catholic character on its next major anniversary:

1. _____

2. _____

3. _____

To celebrate the 130th anniversary of the founding of St. Mary's School (Avilla, IN), the faculty and parents planned a "pioneer enrichment day" for the students. Everyone wore pioneer clothing, including the Sisters who wore the habits they had prior to 1969. The children were divided into pioneer families and went to six different modules including pioneer games, crafts, dancing and music, folk medicine, and a heritage panel presented by a "local historian." Each child also made a square for a pioneer quilt and took a horse-drawn wagon ride around the town. The students then visited a pioneer school enacted by the fourth grade while the cooks prepared an appropriate pioneer lunch. The local TV station featured the day on the 5 o'clock news.

When St. Brendan's School (Mexico, MO) celebrated its 75th anniversary, the school sponsored a special opening liturgy with the Bishop presiding and the former principals—along with former and current parents and students—in attendance. That evening more than 800 people attended a two-hour program consisting of music and dance plus narration that wove together the school's 75-year history with events in the nation's history. Throughout the program, the school community gave special recognition to former pastors, principals, faculty/staff, and alumni. The first student to graduate from St. Brendan's attended and received special congratulations.

Faculty/Student Exchange Programs

Visits to other Catholic schools—whether across town or across the ocean—help students and faculty to realize they are part of something larger than their school. Experiences like these can open eyes to new possibilities and provide opportunities for community building, especially if participants come away with a deeper awareness and understanding of what it means to be "People of God" in a more universal sense. In these ways, faculty/student exchanges promote latitudinal heritage.

Some school communities have initiated short-term exchanges and otherwise network with schools worldwide that were founded by the same religious community. For example, The Prout School (Wakefield, RI) conducted an annual exchange during the 1990s with another Passionist school, Mt. St. Joseph Secondary School, in Bolton, England. Each fall some Prout students traveled to Mt. St. Joseph for two weeks, and, in the spring, vice versa. The students involved experienced some of the similarities as well as the differences with Passionist Catholic schools in another country. The exchange also helped to break down stereotypes.

The Network of Sacred Heart Schools promotes the sense of latitudinal heritage beyond graduation. Principals at Sacred Heart schools issue "passports" in a formal ceremony to graduating seniors to be used in their future travels. With the passport in hand, graduates

Discuss an occasion when members of your school community participated in an exchange/interaction with another school sharing a similar religious heritage:

_____

_____

_____

_____

Identify how might you initiate or strengthen exchanges/interactions with schools sharing a similar religious heritage:

_____

_____

_____

_____

will be welcomed at a school or convent sponsored by the Society of the Religious of the Sacred Heart anywhere in the world.

Catholic Schools Week

Many schools use Catholic Schools Week as a time to celebrate the school's heritage and religious identity. Various school constituencies, including teachers, students, parents, grandparents, and alumni, can be invited to participate in the celebration to honor their collective legacy.

Two Rivers Catholic Central School (Two Rivers, WI) brings its Catholic heritage to life through a 9-year cycle that moves students from the Old Testament to the Church of the future as they progress through their educational program. Each Catholic Schools Week the entire school community participates in an integrated thematic unit based on the time period being studied that year.

Catholic Schools Week affords Catholic educational leaders an excellent opportunity each year to commemorate the school's corporate identity—its latitudinal heritage—and to remember that each Catholic school is part of the largest confederation of private schools in the United States (McDonald, 2000). Catholic elementary schools in Omaha, Nebraska, for example, hold a diocesan Mass for all eighth graders during Catholic Schools Week each year. Looking ahead, perhaps it is time this concept were broadened on a global scale to accentuate the international expanse of Catholic schools and to give students a sense of being part of something larger than their own school community.

St. Michael School (Greenville, PA) begins Catholic Schools Week in the Church with an opening Mass on Sunday at 9:00 a.m. Mass is followed by a breakfast for the teachers and their families. On Monday and Thursday, the school hosts "Grandparents Breakfasts" where grandparents have breakfast with their grandchildren, play games, and learn about the school. Monday evening features a family roller-skating party and, on Tuesday evening, an Open House is held with teachers and students showcasing all of the good things happening in the school. On Wednesday, one student from each class (selected at random by the teacher) is treated to breakfast at Perkins Restaurant with the principal. The local radio station broadcasts from St. Michael's and the eighth graders serve as hosts and interview other students and teachers. The local paper also publishes a full-page feature about St. Michael School. And, students in Grades 5-8 jump rope to raise funds for the American Heart Association. Then, on Thursday, the teachers play the eighth graders in volleyball. Friday features the closing Mass followed by the 8th graders teaching classes. Lastly, there is the Buddy Day Lunch where different classes pair up with one another to get to know everyone in the school. In addition to all of this, some years Catholic Schools Week features a Communion Breakfast for all of the eighth grade students from the

Explain how you utilize Catholic Schools Week to celebrate your school's latitudinal and longitudinal heritage:

_____

_____

_____

_____

Propose three actions you will take to initiate or strengthen your school's commemoration of Catholic Schools Week in light of its religious heritage:

1. _____

2. _____

3. _____

four Catholic elementary schools in Mercer County.

Alumni and Intergenerational Outreach

Having alumni representation on the teaching staff is an important way for schools to bridge the past with the present. In a sense, alumni/ae teachers embody school heritage, in the same way generations of vowed men and women religious who came before them did.

To reach out to older members of the local community, St. Anne School (Bismarck, ND) created an "intergenerational" program. The principal put an advertisement in the church bulletin requesting any interested retired person to adopt a class at the school. The response was gratifying and resulted in each class having at least one adopted sponsor. The program now boasts wonderful intergenerational friendships. The adopted sponsors are always welcome at the school and participate in school activities in a variety of ways.

Sacred Heart School (East Grand Forks, MN) is a small Catholic school in a small town supported by one parish. This pre-Kindergarten through 12th grade school is over 80 years old, and the founding parish is now over 100 years old. Many of current students have parents who attended Sacred Heart and some have grandparents who attended the school. This tradition builds moral support for the next generation of students and the school's boosters. During Catholic Schools Week, families participate in a number of activities including a school liturgy, "Muffin Munching Morning," and a sixth grade versus parents basketball game. Alumni support is promoted with the students writing alumni and asking them to share their memories of Sacred Heart.

In the small Nebraska community of North Platte, most students leave North Platte Catholic after graduation to pursue "fame and fortune" elsewhere. But, they carry the values and faith experiences of their bygone school days with them. The journey "home" often culminates when graduates return to bury a parent or sibling. At North Platte Catholic, it is a specific element of the educator's ministry to see that no graduate returns for a family funeral without the faculty being represented at the wake service, funeral, and burial. Many times the faculty member present may be the only person there "just for" a graduate. This "comforting of the sorrowful" and "burying of the dead"—intended as a ministry to the graduate—has actually been a tremendous blessing to the faculty who experience a special grace by sharing their faith this way.

Chapter Summary

By attending to school history, Catholic educational leaders create strong cultures whose members do not forget their past. As Catholic educational leaders identify the significance of the school's religious heritage, they provide the school's members a sense of

Reflect on your school's alumni and intergenerational outreach.

- *How do you actively reconnect alumni with your school's religious heritage and mission?*
- *What opportunities do you provide for current students to interact with alumni in an effort to build a "community of memory" and a "community of hope"?*

In light of your school's alumni and intergenerational outreach activities, suggest three ways to highlight your school's religious mission through these activities:

1. _____
2. _____
3. _____

rootedness in and belonging to something that is more important and enduring than the self.

It is incumbent upon Catholic educational leaders, then, to help their schools continuously rediscover, renew, and, if necessary, refound their religious and historical heritage. As architects of Catholic culture, Catholic educational leaders invariably transform the school from a "community of memory" into a "community of hope" by building strong and vibrant Catholic school cultures.

Chapter 9

• Cultural players...

Cultural players form the cast of characters who serve as a group's informal communication and culture building network, the "carriers" (Deal & Kennedy, 1982, p. 15) of culture. These individuals might not have titles appearing on the organizational chart but this "hidden hierarchy" (p. 85) wields influence just the same. Informal leaders can use personal influence to build up or tear down an organization.

Leaders must attend to these realities and forge alliances with these informal leaders in order to pursue organizational goals. While this requires a good deal of persuasive ability, these efforts pay off when various subcultures support and endorse the organization's culture instead of forming a counterculture. Furthermore, when leaders realize that culture is not constructed by one individual, they place a premium on socializing and acculturating other cultural players into the organization and, as such, function as architects of organizational culture.

Catholic culture...

Many groups and individuals in the Catholic Church transmit religious heritage informally. The institutes of vowed men and women religious have socialized generations into Catholic culture, especially through the Catholic schools. Likewise, the Knights of Columbus and numerous women's sodalities have functioned as kinship groups and cabals, offering members opportunities to experience various dimensions of Catholic life. Television is a relatively new agent of socialization that has provided a forum for Catholics to function as storytellers, including Bishop Fulton Sheen during the 1950s and Mother Angelica in the 1990s. Likewise, Catholic magazines and newspapers, as well as authors who write about topics that enliven spiritual growth and spark the Catholic imagination, serve as carriers of Catholic culture.

school culture...

Like other organizations, schools are not immune from organizational politics, for there exists in every school an informal underground network that serves as an information pipeline, memory bank, and forum where people negotiate.

Deal and Peterson (1999) identify the cast of major characters in this informal network according to five categories. One category— heroes and heroines—has already been treated (see Chapter 4). The other four categories include priests/priestesses, storytellers, gossips, and spies.

First, there are the priests/priestesses, individuals who have been around for a while and are respected by their peers. They may or may not be identified on the school's organizational chart, but they provide links to the school's past. Through the force of their personalities, priests and priestesses preside over the school's culture as "keepers of the values" (p. 56).

Savvy principals know these people can be "breakers" or "brokers" of school culture, "allies to be won over to the cause" when change is proposed. If these individuals are not won over, they may quickly become saboteurs. Thus, to gain support for a proposed change, principals work nimbly with these individuals to gain their "blessing" for the initiatives and to allow them to be the standard bearers of change.

The second category includes storytellers, the people whose tenure makes it possible for them to convey core values by telling and retelling stories. In this way, "an institution's memory is transmitted from one generation to another" (Johnston, 1987, p. 81). Because storytellers possess the school's collective memory, they serve as its memory banks, and therefore, as carriers of school culture.

Teachers who are alumni/ae of the school link the school's past with its present by standing before their students as the type of person the school produces. In *Dead Poets Society,* for example, as a graduate of Welton, Mr. Keating once sat in the same desks occupied by his students. Sharing kindred experiences created a symbiotic bond between Keating and his students.

The third category of cultural players includes gossips. Justifiably or not, the "Faculty Room" functions as "Gossip Central" or like an Internet "chat room." While it is true that the faculty room can serve positive purposes, the faculty room can easily devolve into a meeting place where "toxic" energy abounds. This is particularly dangerous for new teachers who must take care not to allow themselves to be drawn into negativity by veteran teachers who have an axe to grind or who are simply burned out (Keller, 1999).

Spies constitute the fourth category. These people observe and pass information. The network of spies found in schools points to the fact that many negotiations and deals transpire within a school's underground network.

Two matters are noteworthy. First, the school's informal network is not limited to teachers. New principals quickly learn about other participants in the informal network, for example, parents, alumni, board members, and students. In a school's ordinary day-to-day operations, custodians and secretaries also function as cultural players. Because custodians ordinarily are not authority figures, they witness activities that administrators and teachers normally are not privy to. In addition, secretaries are invaluable cultural players because their informal network extends beyond the school's property lines. At the same time, however, these cultural players can become impediments to change. The principal needs to work with these individuals—or replace them if necessary—to effect a school culture that represents what the school says it is.

Lastly, it is the principal's job to understand and work with the school's informal network and its politics. As crass and unseemly as this work may be, adept principals forge alliances with the school's informal leaders and monitor their communications network. In the final analysis, it is the principal's job to "fill the network with stories of success, achievement, and devotion to the school's core values" (Johnston, 1995, p. 15).

Catholic school culture...

Because Catholic school culture is built on the premise that Christianity is a way of life and as such must be reinforced and modeled daily, teachers are key cultural players. Over three decades ago, the Second Vatican Council noted this, asserting: "Teachers must remember that it depends chiefly on them whether the Catholic school achieves its purpose" (1965a/1996, #8). Twelve years later, the Congregation for Catholic Education affirmed this vision: "By their witness and their behavior teachers are of the first importance to impart a distinctive character to Catholic schools" (1977, #78). While some might prefer that religion teachers bear responsibility for the school's religious mission, the National Conference of Catholic Bishops (1976) responds that "… all [teachers] share in the educational ministry, not just those specifically assigned to 'teach religion' " (p. 4). The ministry of teaching in a Catholic school makes each teacher a cultural player, a responsibility transcending all disciplines and including all teachers.

In the Catholic school setting, then, teaching is relational on several levels, including the spiritual. Reflecting the thinking of Pope Pius XII, Jacobs (1996) calls this encounter between teacher and student "an intimate communication between souls" (p. 37). The student-teacher relationship in the culture of the Catholic school is permeated by Christian personalism, an encounter whereby "young men and women come to recognize the Lord Jesus living and acting in their midst" (p. 38).

In the final analysis, it is the quality of the spiritual encounters between students and teachers that will be the hallmark of a "Gospel culture." Since "only women and men of faith can share faith…" (National Conference of Catholic Bishops, 1979, #207), it is incumbent upon Catholic educational leaders to recruit, employ, evaluate, and retain teachers who will make this important difference.

CULTURAL BUILDING PLAN:
SOCIALIZE FACULTY AND STAFF
TO GOSPEL VALUES AND RELIGIOUS MISSION

Where cultural players and the transmission of culture are concerned, theorists emphasize the importance of socialization (Deal & Peterson, 1990, 1999; Schein, 1992; Trice & Beyer, 1993; Sergiovanni, 1995a). Trice and Beyer (1993) define socialization as "the process by

---

Reflecting upon "Christian personalism" in your experience and your school's way of life:
- *Can you identify an instance where you experienced "an intimate communication between souls"?*

_____

_____

_____

- *Check the statement that best describes your school's culture*:

____ *"Student faith formation is the responsibility of every teacher."*

____ *"Student faith formation is the responsibility of religion teachers."*

Identify three actions that will deepen your faculty's commitment to teaching as ministry and/or skill at relating to students on the level of "Christian personalism":

1. _____

2. _____

3. _____

---

which persons are inculcated with substance and forms of a culture" (p. 129).

When religious communities staffed Catholic schools, socialization of teachers occurred naturally as the religious communities went about their work. This built-in formation no longer exists. Therefore, it is imperative for Catholic educational leaders—as architects of Catholic culture—to place a premium on the formal and ongoing socialization of the cultural players in Catholic schools through recruitment, selection, formation, and evaluation.

Faculty/Staff Selection

Without doubt, one of the most important aspects of a principal's job involves hiring competent and qualified teachers. Since it is the quality of the interaction between students and teachers that distinguishes a good school, it is the quality of the teachers that will make or break a school. In a study of principals considered to be effective in shaping strong school cultures, Deal and Peterson (1999) concluded that a strategy common to all centered on the careful selection of faculty.

Where Catholic schools are concerned, the school's religious mission adds an additional wrinkle. In the eyes of the Church, Catholic schoolteachers are public ministers who "fulfill a specific Christian vocation and share an equally specific participation in the mission of the Church…" (Congregation for Catholic Education, 1997/1998, #19). If Catholic schools are to fulfill their religious purpose, this aspect cannot be undermined when selecting new faculty. Catholic educational leaders must place a premium on recruiting "teachers with appropriate qualifications in view of the Catholic school's apostolic goals and character" (National Conference of Catholic Bishops, 1979, #215).

As burdensome and time-consuming as the hiring process is, Catholic educational leaders would do well to consider the opportunity to hire new faculty a blessing rather than a curse. First—for the newly hired—the hiring process establishes the principal as the school's formal leader from the first day. More importantly, the hiring process allows the principal to build a faculty culture informed about and eager to participate in promoting the school's mission.

In addition to assessing a candidate's educational philosophy, Catholic educational leaders should engage the candidate in a candid discussion about the school's religious mission. To be effective, it helps if the candidate has had an opportunity to study the school's mission statement prior to this interview. During the discussion, the principal should make discrete inquiry into the place of faith in the candidate's personal life and what contributions the candidate might make to promote the school's religious mission.

McBride (1983) and Newton (1979) offer interview questions that focus on the willingness of candidates to participate in the Catholic school's religious mission and which help in assessing each candidate's personal and professional religious attitudes. Figure 14 lists nine questions Catholic educational leaders might use to assess candidates for

---

Figure 14.
Religious Mission and Personal Faith: Sample Questions for Interviewing Applicants

- What is your image of God?
- What role does Jesus play in your life?
- When do you pray? With what style of prayer are you most comfortable?
- In what ways do you live out your faith?
- Are you Catholic? To what parish do you belong?
- Did you attend Catholic schools? If yes, in what ways was it a positive or negative experience?
- Why did you apply to this school?
- What is appealing about teaching in a Catholic school?
- In what concrete ways do you think you could contribute to the religious mission of this school?

---

teaching positions.

Perhaps the most systematic approach to hiring Catholic school-teachers is the "Catholic School Teacher Perceiver Interview" (CTSPI) developed by Gallup, Inc. (formerly SRI). Training is necessary, however, if principals are to use the CTSPI effectively when assessing a candidate's potential.

Some Catholic educational leaders have developed hiring and interviewing protocols that focus on the school's religious mission. For the principal of Mount St. Charles Academy (Woonsocket, RI), professional qualifications do matter, but essential to developing the sense of community which is the heart of Catholic education is the ability to share and nurture faith. In the hiring process, then, applicants explore their understanding of the school's mission, their personal comfort with prayer and liturgy, and something of their faith life. This sets the context for the principal to articulate the school's mission and expectations of faculty:

- to participate daily in prayer with the students in their homeroom and elsewhere;
- to share in and support the liturgical life of the school; and,
- to be actively involved in the spiritual life of the school.

While it is easy to find a teacher, it is more difficult to open a teacher's eyes to the wonder of education, to open the teacher's heart

---

Recall your most recent experience with hiring a new member of staff.
- *What materials did you provide each candidate that explained the religious mission of Catholic schools and the ministry of teaching, in general, or as it is lived out at your school?*

_____
_____
_____

Identity materials that should be provided in the future:

1. _____
2. _____
3. _____

How did you engage each candidate in a discussion about personal spirituality and the contributions each candidate might make to the school's religious mission?

List additional interview questions that you will ask in the future:

1. _____
2. _____
3. _____

What expectations do you discuss with each teacher candidate relative to their role in furthering your school's religious mission?

Cite additional expectations to address in the future:

1. _____
2. _____
3. _____

Describe ways in which your faculty/staff orientation program addresses religious mission, charisms, and teaching as ministry:

_____

_____

_____

_____

Suggest actions you will take to make religious mission, charisms, and teaching as ministry more prominent in your orientation program:

1. _____
2. _____
3. _____

to the students and their difficulties, and to open a teacher's mind to new directions and challenges in teaching. On the surface, many of the questions asked may not be different from other interviews but, as many applicants are closely matched in terms of professional qualifications, the importance of character, of openness, of flexibility, of a student focus, and of a spirituality become more telling. A candidate's responses usually speak volumes. They range from "Oh, I'm comfortable with that" or "No problem" to visions of education that include the spiritual—for themselves and their students. This is a revealing element in the interview because it provides answers the question, "Will this person build with us the community we aspire to be?"

Faculty/Staff Orientation

Once hired, new faculty and staff should experience a formal orientation that, among other things, addresses religious mission.

At St. Francis Central Catholic School (Morgantown, WV), new teachers find support and strengthen their skills through formal orientation programs before the school year begins. At these sessions, new personnel acquaint themselves with the school's philosophy and mission, the Parent/Student and Faculty handbooks, and general expectations. In addition, the principal assigns all new teachers to a faculty mentor, who takes special interest in the new faculty member's professional development. The mentor provides guidance, support, and communicates openly with the new teacher about questions or issues that arise.

The Catholic School Department of the Diocese of Worcester (MA) takes a diocesan approach to new teacher orientation, one that has evolved into a three-year program. Originally, new teacher orientation included one segment about religious mission designed to introduce new Catholic school personnel to the charisms of the religious communities that founded and staffed the schools for so many decades. In small groups, participants focused on two questions: 1) How are these charisms experienced in the school community today? 2) What do school personnel need to pay attention to if they are to ensure that these charisms will continue to permeate school life? Commenting on how new teachers receive this session, an associate superintendent writes: "We are constantly amazed by their fascination with the idea of a founding charism and their eagerness to embrace the heritage to which they have been called. To a person, each evaluation speaks of the delight and renewed sense of mission and pride following this session" (P. Halpin, personal communication, June, 1999). The segment about charism now is one session of the more extensive three-year program.

Faculty/Staff Formation

Asking a teacher or staff member to participate in the school's religious mission without proper formation would be akin to asking someone without any background or training to teach math.

Recognizing the Catholic school teacher as a key player in the evangelizing mission of Catholic schools, Church documents have stressed the need to prepare teachers to fulfill this role. *The Catholic School* declares: "By their witness and their behavior teachers are of the first importance to impart a distinctive character to Catholic schools. It is, therefore, indispensable to ensure their continuing formation through some form of suitable pastoral provision" (Congregation for Catholic Education, 1977, #78). Five years later, *Lay Catholics in Schools* expounded on the need for systematic formation and support if lay Catholic educators are to become full participants in the educational mission of the Church. The document states that "all too frequently, lay Catholics have not had a religious formation that is equal to their general cultural, and, most especially, professional formation" (Congregation for Catholic Education, 1982, #60). To prepare Catholic school teachers for their unique educational role, formation must attend to both "personal sanctification" and "apostolic mission." Professional development, like religious formation, must be ongoing (#68). Although *Lay Catholics in Schools* recommends that centers for teacher formation be created to help teachers engage students in a dialogue between faith and culture, the document specifies what teachers should expect from their school, and ultimately, their leaders:

> As a part of its mission, one element proper to the Catholic school is solicitous care for the permanent professional and religious formation of its lay members. Lay people should be able to look to the school for the orientation and the assistance that they need, including the willingness to make time available when this is needed. Formation is indispensable; without it, the school will wander further and further away from its objectives. (#79)

Catholic educational leaders around the country have responded to the need for faculty religious development in a variety of creative ways. Commonly, the religious dimension of professional development includes a personal spirituality component and/or a public ministry component.

In some schools, principals have teachers gather regularly for prayer. The principal of St. Margaret Mary School (Omaha, NE), starts each day with faculty morning prayer. Faculty attendance for this five minute prayer ritual each day is voluntary. Teachers and administrators lead prayer on a rotating basis. The principal reports that "approximately 50% of the faculty attends on any given day" (J. Andrews, personal communication, January, 1997). The principal at St. Joan of Arc School (Boca Raton, FL) convenes the faculty every Monday after school for a prayer service led by individual teachers.

The 1982 Congregation for Catholic Education document "Lay Catholics in Schools: Witnesses to Faith" challenges Catholic educational leaders to demonstrate "solicitous care" in providing for spiritual growth and faith community among the school's faculty/staff.

Describe a situation where you demonstrated solicitous care.

_____

_____

_____

_____

Propose three plans to enhance spiritual growth and building faith community among faculty/staff:

1. _____
2. _____
3. _____

Describe how you demonstrate "solicitous care" in providing your faculty/staff the resources and skills they need to carry out their public ministry:

_____

_____

_____

_____

At St. James School (Perris, CA), the principal incorporates prayer and religious development into the regularly scheduled faculty meetings. Each teacher takes a turn in preparing and leading faculty in prayer. To aid in religious development, the faculty might read a common text to facilitate growth and group discussion. Recently, the faculty reflected on the Apostolic Letter, *Tertio Millennio Adveniente*, in preparation for Great Jubilee Year 2000. According to the principal, "The teachers have often expressed gratitude for the ongoing formation and opportunities for spiritual growth available at St. James. There is enthusiasm on the part of the faculty to be involved in faith sharing at our meetings" (M. Coleman, personal communication, January, 1997).

To be responsive to the mission of the Catholic school, the principal of All Souls Catholic School (South San Francisco, CA) provides the following opportunities for spiritual growth and formation:

- The faculty and staff gather daily before school during Advent and Lent for a communal prayer experience.
- Every August, the pastor and faculty go on an overnight retreat. This retreat is the opening session for the faculty faith development program the principal incorporates into the year's religion in-service meetings.
- In order to create an environment, climate, and spirit conducive to an optimal moral education program, the principal developed a faculty Moral Education Handbook.

The principal notes: "Through these endeavors we hope to provide an environment in our school which facilitates the development of a child's moral character so that young people have the opportunity to make suitable, ethical choices based upon Christian teachings" (E. Gorman, personal communication, January, 1997).

Many Catholic educational leaders utilize NCEA's *Sharing the Faith* program as a two- or three- year approach to faculty faith formation. This program fosters personal spirituality, builds faculty faith community, and deepens faculty commitment to and participation in the school's religious mission.

Some Catholic school leaders fold their faculty religious development program into one sponsored and/or mandated by their diocese. As part of the requirements for contract renewal at St. Joan of Arc School (Boca Raton, FL), all teachers must obtain their Advanced Catechist Certification (if they are catechists) or their Basic Catechist Certification (if they are not catechists). Every staff member must take 10 hours of theology to update their certificates. Teachers also participate in the Annual Diocesan Catechetical Day. Echoing the sentiments of many Catholic educational leaders, a veteran teacher at Joan of Arc School writes: "We are constantly working at building community among faculty. The Catholic formation of teachers is essentially an ongoing process" (L. Davidson, personal communication, January, 1997).

At St. Raphael School (Louisville, KY), the religion curriculum team has developed guidelines for promoting and maintaining the school's Catholic identity. Among others, these guidelines include reminders for all teachers to participate fully in Church services, the rules of Church etiquette all are to follow, and the values all should be teaching. In addition, the principal and curriculum team provide teachers with Church teaching from the new catechism concerning all "touchy" issues. Furthermore, the weekly "MEMOS" and newsletters contain sections devoted to Catholic identity. Both publications provide teachers and parents suggestions about how to promote the school's values.

When public ministry and classroom instruction intersect as a result of focused faculty religious development, teachers more effectively communicate the school's purpose as a *Catholic* school. It is in these moments that Catholic educational leaders can take great pride and experience profound personal and professional satisfaction. The principal of Holy Rosary School (Duluth, MN) expresses it this way: "It is very heartening to see a teacher address a classroom issue in terms of the spiritual applications that would help direct students to choose what is good. These types of encounters between teacher and student create a strong basic foundation in values that has become the hallmark of Holy Rosary School" (P. D. Vekich, personal communication, January, 1997).

Faculty/Staff Evaluation

In secular as well as religious schools, principals evaluate each teacher's instructional skills as well as student academic achievement. Although not everyone agrees about how teachers should be evaluated, few object to the idea of evaluating teachers, in principle.

Because the religious mission distinguishes Catholic schools from their secular counterparts and since "… all [teachers] share in the educational ministry, not just those specifically assigned to 'teach religion' " (National Conference of Catholic Bishops, 1976, p. 4), it is incumbent upon Catholic educational leaders to evaluate their teachers in light of the school's religious mission. To deal with this challenge, Newton (1978) proposes a comprehensive, three-stage faculty growth plan that encompasses selection, development, *and* evaluation of personnel. For Newton, a teacher's contributions to the school's religious mission should be evaluated alongside the teacher's contributions to the school's academic mission.

At Creighton Prep (Omaha, NE), the teaching contract and evaluation instruments are linked to the school's total educational mission. The contract spells out specific teacher responsibilities and makes reference to important documents such as the *Profile of the Ig-*

Reflect upon the role that religious mission plays in faculty/staff evaluation.

- *What are your school's expectations of faculty/staff in terms of responsibility for carrying forward the school's religious mission? Cite school document(s) where these responsibilities are delineated:*

_____

_____

_____

_____

- *Describe the evaluation processes and instruments used to evaluate faculty/staff in light of the school's religious mission:*

_____

_____

_____

_____

Outline a plan for strengthening the connection between your school's religious mission and faculty staff evaluation:

1. _____
2. _____
3. _____
4. _____

Grade the religious mission dimension of your school's faculty/staff evaluation scheme from "A" to "F" in terms of the following considerations:

_____ *Expectations are clearly written.*
_____ *Concrete behaviors and activities that meet expectations are provided.*
_____ *There is flexibility to accommodate a diverse faculty/staff.*
_____ *Self-evaluation is part of the evaluation process.*

Identify actions you will take to improve your school's grades:

1. _____
2. _____
3. _____

natian Educator, the *Core Values of Creighton Prep*, and the *Profile of the Graduate at Graduation*. From the moment each teacher arrives, one knows what is expected. Then, faculty in-service programs often revolve around the principles outlined in these important documents.

The *Profile of the Ignatian Educator* spells out five dimensions that characterize the educator in a Jesuit school: intellectually competent, religious, open to growth, loving, and committed to justice. The evaluation instrument is also divided into these five categories, each listing specific teaching behaviors, attitudes, and involvements. Teachers are rated accordingly.

Ignatian identity is weighted heavily in the faculty performance evaluation. All teachers are expected to be concerned with their students' spiritual development. All teachers are required to participate in at least one spiritual activity which can include leading student retreats, participating in service projects, and leading student prayer groups.

During each of the first five years of teaching, the principal visits the classroom and schedules a meeting with the teacher. The principal uses the evaluation instrument, associated documents, and contractual items as the basis for the annual performance assessment. To write the formal evaluation, the principal also relies on feedback gathered from the Directors of Athletics, Counseling, Campus Ministry, the teacher's Department Chair, and students—all relative to the teacher's performance in the five dimensions. This provides a well-rounded view of the teacher's contributions to the school's total mission.

After the fifth year, if the teacher has established a pattern of good performance and has completed a masters degree or 36 hours beyond the bachelors degree, tenure will be granted and the extensive evaluative process will occur every three years thereafter. However, the principal continues to formulate an annual written evaluation.

As Catholic educational leaders incorporate the religious dimension into faculty/staff evaluation, they should take into account the following considerations:

- School expectations and assessment measures regarding faculty/ staff contribution to religious mission should be spelled out in the Faculty Handbook.
- School expectations and assessment measures should be as concrete as possible. For example, a school expectation that teachers pray before each class is an observable behavior. Likewise, a school expectation that social studies teachers integrate Catholic social teaching into the curriculum can be documented through lesson plans and classroom visits.
- School expectations should be flexible to accommodate the reality that each educator is at a different place in his/her faith journey.
- Faculty/staff evaluation in terms of the religious dimension of school life should include a self-evaluation component to promote reflection, conversation, and growth.

It is very likely that even now, in the more than two decades following the publication of Newton's (1978) proposal, faculty/staff evaluation in light of religious mission is still more the exception than the rule. Developing instruments and processes for faculty/staff evaluation remains unfinished business for Catholic educational leaders (Cook, 1999).

Chapter Summary

Cultural players are the cast of characters who serve as a group's informal communication and culture building network. In essence, they are the human carriers of culture. These are the breakers and brokers of culture who may or may not appear on an organizational chart.

Teachers are key cultural players. But, because Catholic school culture encompasses a religious dimension, teachers in Catholic schools are the key cultural players who must embrace this religious mission if Catholic schools are to realize their goals. As architects of Catholic culture, Catholic educational leaders must give priority to selecting, developing, and evaluating faculty/staff with regard to Gospel values and religious mission.

Chapter 10

- ## Architects of catholic culture:
  ## Seven norms for Catholic educational leaders

A one-half page newspaper advertisement printed in the Saturday morning edition of the *Omaha World-Herald* announced the opening of a new science wing at a local Jesuit high school and invited the public to attend its dedication ceremonies. Perusing the ad, Catholic educational leaders—in their role as architects of Catholic culture—would scan it, inquiring: "What message, if any, does this ad convey about the school's religious mission, especially to those unfamiliar with the school?"

This simple but incisive question directs attention to the central argument of *Architects of Catholic Culture*: If Catholic educational leaders are to fulfill the purpose for which Catholic schools exist, these women and men must be conscious of and attentive to what is truly distinctive about these schools, namely, a distinctive Catholic culture.

Strong and effective organizations invariably possess cultures that provide a more meaningful way of life for members (Schein, 1992). The culture of Roman Catholicism, for example, offers a unique vision about human existence and a configuration of core commitments that enable its members to bring that vision to fruition. This vision and configuration of core commitments is what distinguishes Catholics, their experience of God, and their spiritual imagination from members of other religious traditions. The most effective and authentic Catholic schools, then, provide members an experience of a way of life that springs from this Catholic vision, transmits the configuration of core commitments to its members, and captures their spiritual imagination.

The purpose of the Catholic school springs from the belief that Christianity is not solely an idea or a creed but also, and more substantively, a way of life. As such, Christianity in a Catholic school must be lived, reinforced, and modeled each and every day. Just as students learn foreign languages through immersion into differing language systems, students in Catholic schools learn Christianity by "doing" Christianity. What distinguishes Catholic school communities from their public or private counterparts, then, is that each school's culture—what it is and how it functions—is intentionally related to Scripture and Tradition.

In this sense, "Catholic school culture" is really "Catholic school life," a way of life as distinct educationally as the American way of life is distinct nationally. Rooted in Christ, who is "the Way, the Truth, and the Life" (John 14:6), Catholic school culture is an all-encompassing "way of life," a Gospel-based creed and code, and a Catholic vision that provides inspiration and identity, is shaped over time, and is passed from one generation to the next through devices that capture the Catholic imagination such as symbols and traditions. Whether Catholic educational leaders invoke official terms—like "permeation," "synthesis," and "integration"—to underscore the all-encompassing faith dimension of the Catholic school way of life, Catholic school culture is a "Gospel Culture." A school is authentically Catholic, then, when a Gospel culture animates everything that transpires in the school.

This definition of Catholic school culture implies that Catholic school culture does not happen by itself. Rather, architects of Catholic culture intentionally design and plan and they nurture and develop distinctively Catholic school cultures. Not only does this "architect" metaphor stand in stark contrast to other, more predominant metaphors emphasizing the more routine and functional dimensions of school leadership; this metaphor also directs attention to the more creative and artistic dimensions of the Catholic educational leader's professional and ministerial roles within the Catholic school community.

Because architects of Catholic culture exercise creativity and artistry as they contemplate and enact role requirements, there is no "one best way" to identify what individual Catholic educational leaders will do. Instead, seven norms provide guidelines for them to contemplate just how they will function as architects of Catholic culture.

> **Norm 1**: *Architects of Catholic culture act with "intentionality" to nurture the Catholic imagination and to connect everything in the school to Christ, the Gospel, and the Catholic vision.*

Identify how Norm 1 evidences itself in your Catholic educational leadership practice:

_____

_____

_____

_____

Pinpoint three actions you will take so that Norm 1 becomes more fully evident in your Catholic educational leadership practice:

1. _____
2. _____
3. _____

Gone are the days when religious culture in Catholic schools happened by osmosis due primarily to the pervasive presence of religious congregations in schools. Because Catholic educational leaders and faculty/staff today are a more heterogeneous group less likely to have benefited from the implicit formation provided by the members of the religious congregations, this generation's Catholic educational leaders must act with "intentionality" when it comes to preserving and enhancing religious culture in Catholic schools. Schuttloffel (1999) calls this more explicit form of intentional formation "contemplative practice" (p. 67).

Whether Catholic educational leaders are discerning the design of something as simple as an advertisement or something as complex as new directions in curriculum and programs or faculty hiring, it is as architects of Catholic culture that they intentionally approach decision making in light of Gospel values and the school's religious mission. In other words, architects of Catholic culture systematically and deliberately "connect" everything in the school with its religious mission. In the decision-making process, the simple question "How will this decision or activity reflect or enhance Gospel values and the school's religious mission?" provides the focus for architects of Catholic culture.

> **Norm 2**: *Architects of Catholic culture consciously endeavor to build a multicultural school culture.*

Vatican II underscored the universal and global character of the Catholic Church and the duty of Catholics to build a more just and peaceful world. In *Church in the Modern World*, the Council affirms:

> By its nature and mission the Church is universal in that it is not committed to any one culture or to any political, economic or social system....With this in view the Church calls upon its members and upon all people to put aside, in the family spirit of the children of God, all conflict between nations and races and to build up the internal strength of just human associations. (Vatican Council II, 1965d/1996, #42)

The Council gives particular emphasis to the multicultural and international dimension of the Christian faith that is uniquely and especially Catholic.

In the spirit of Vatican II, Catholic educational leaders underscore universality and inclusivity as core values animating the school community. These women and men step up efforts to increase cultural awareness among the school's members. These Catholic educational leaders also emphasize the duty of Catholics to work toward cultural harmony by inculcating in faculty/staff and student body the desire to build a more just and peaceful world. Lastly, these Catholic educational leaders recognize that Catholic imagination, though distinct from other faith traditions, is not monolithic. Therefore, these Catholic educational leaders design and build a multicultural religious culture in their schools and, as architects of Catholic culture, engage in these and many other efforts intended to reinforce the truly catholic nature of Catholicism.

Norm 3: *Architects of Catholic culture utilize common building blocks to develop building plans to support and promote the school's purpose.*

Architects of Catholic Culture affirms that strong organizational cultures share an architecture consisting of common building blocks. For example, even though nations like the United States, corporations like Disney, and schools like Harvard University exist in different arenas and serve different purposes, the strong culture each exudes gives evidence of some common elements or "building blocks." Architects of Catholic culture recognize the "transferability" of these cultural building blocks and the building plans designed from them.

This notion of transferability has direct implications for Catholic educational leadership practice. For example, as the master builders of religious culture in their schools, architects of Catholic culture adapt these building blocks to design building plans in a wide variety of ways, each of which promotes a distinctively Catholic school culture (Figure 15).

Identify how Norm 2 is evident in your Catholic educational leadership practice:

_____

_____

_____

_____

Cite three actions to ensure that Norm 2 will more fully characterize your Catholic educational leadership practice:

1. _____

2. _____

3. _____

Identify how Norm 3 evidences itself in your Catholic educational leadership practice:

_____

_____

_____

_____

List three actions you will take so that Norm 3 becomes more fully evident in your Catholic educational leadership practice:

1. _____
2. _____
3. _____

Figure 15.
Building Blocks and Building Plans for Architects of Catholic Culture

- *Building Block*: **Core Beliefs & Values**
  Building Plan: Identify and integrate core religious beliefs and values using the mission statement
  and   resources.

- *Building Block*: **Heroes and Heroines**
  Building Plan: Honor heroes and heroines who exemplify Gospel values and religious mission.

- *Building Block*: **Symbols**
  Building Plan: Create and display a symbol system reflecting Gospel values and religious mission.

- *Building Block*: **Ritual Tradition**
  Building Plan: Nurture prayer and worship through routine rituals. Use ceremonial rituals to showcase Gospel values and religious mission.

- *Building Block*: **Human Communication**
  Building Plan: Use language to communicate Gospel values and religious mission. Tell stories that   communicate Gospel values and religious   mission.

- *Building Block*: **History**
  Building Plan: Rediscover the school's religious and historical heritage.

- *Building Block*: **Cultural Players**
  Building Plan: Socialize faculty and staff to Gospel values and religious mission.

Norm 4:   *Architects of Catholic culture assist the school community to identify and develop its unique charism.*

With so many competing societal values and opinions whirling about, it is easy for people in Catholic schools to lose focus. Architects of Catholic culture, however, utilize a "blueprint" of the Catholic vision to keep the school's members focused on the institution's religious mission. Because the Catholic vision is so expansive and all-encompassing (McBrien, 1994; Hellwig, 1995; Groome, 1996, 1998), architects of Catholic culture prudently focus the attention of the school community on a few core convictions.

A look at schools sponsored by religious congregations proves instructive in this regard because Catholic schools associated with religious congregations appear to exhibit stronger and more cohesive school cultures. The sharper focus and clearer purpose these schools exhibit can be attributed to the core values that flow from the sponsoring congregation's charism. For example, in the *Omaha World-Herald* advertisement announcing the new science wing at a Jesuit high school, the school's president connected the capital campaign with the Ignatian charism of *magis*. He noted: "Our commitment to the Omaha community is to continue to strive for the '*magis*,' an ever-increasing level of excellence as described by St. Ignatius some four hundred years ago" (*Omaha World-Herald*, March 11, 2000, p. 12).

Charism is a gift that God gives freely to individuals. It is a divine gift to be used for the common good (Nardoni, 1993). While many associate this term exclusively with the Pentecost event, the New Testament uses the word charism more expansively, 17 times in all. Of those 17 instances, St. Paul used charism 14 times (p. 69), likening the relationship between individual charisms and the good of the community with the body's dependence on the function of each of its parts (Romans 12:4-6).

In the case of religious congregations, a particular charism is most oftentimes rooted in the person of the founder/foundress (Renfro, 1986). More recently, however, the meaning associated with a congregation's charism has been expanded to include the congregation's spiritual gifts as a corporate entity. These have been manifest in the congregation's living culture in the decades and centuries following the death of the founder/foundress (McDonough, 1993).

Vatican documents recognize the pervasive influence of a religious congregation's charism on the character of the schools sponsored by religious congregations. The Congregation for Catholic Education (1982) states: "Certain elements will be characteristic of all Catholic schools. But these can be expressed in a variety of ways: often enough, the concrete expression will correspond to the specific charism of the religious institute that founded the school and continues to direct it" (#39). In many instances, a religious congregation's unique charism has exerted a profound influence, especially upon the school's distinctiveness and effectiveness. Yet, faced with the reality of the declining number of religious, the challenge for the leaders of schools sponsored by religious communities—as architects of Catholic culture—is to investigate new mechanisms for "charism transmission" in an increasingly diverse school community (Hilton, 1997).

Following the example and experience of schools sponsored by religious congregations, architects of Catholic culture identify and develop their school's unique "community charism" (Clark, 1998, pp. 117, 141). Drawn from Gospel values (e.g., community, service, hospi-

Identify how Norm 4 is evident in your Catholic educational leadership practice:

_____

_____

_____

_____

Pinpoint three actions you will take so that Norm 4 more fully characterizes your Catholic educational leadership practice:

1. _____
2. _____
3. _____

Identify how Norm 5 evidences itself in your Catholic educational leadership practice:

_____

_____

_____

_____

Specify three actions you will take so that Norm 5 becomes more fully evident in your Catholic educational leadership practice:

1. _____
2. _____
3. _____

tality) and Catholic teaching (e.g., human dignity, social responsibility), a Catholic school community's charism focuses and contextualizes the Catholic vision for each school, increasing the vision's relevance for the members of that school community. The American Bishops support this approach in *To Teach as Jesus Did*, noting: "While the Christian purpose of the Catholic school must always be clearly evident, no one form is prescribed for it" (National Conference of Catholic Bishops, 1972, #123 cited in Clark, p. 141).

Architects of Catholic culture, then, use the religious term *charism* rather than the secular term *core values* to link the school's general educational purpose with its distinctive religious mission.

Norm 5: *Architects of Catholic culture view the Catholic school as an "educational project" whose religious mission and culture demands ongoing attention and renewal.*

Since the 1970s, Church documents have highlighted the theme of renewal for Catholic schools (Congregation for Catholic Education, 1977, 1982, 1988, 1997/1998). The use of the term "educational project" (1997/1998, #4) bespeaks the Congregation's idea that Catholic schools are not "finished projects" but "works in progress." In no uncertain terms, the Congregation stridently declares: "It must never be forgotten that the school itself is always in the process of being created..." (1982, #69).

Architects of Catholic culture work to "institutionalize" Catholic culture by embedding Gospel values and religious mission into the school's culture. This is how architects of Catholic culture ensure that the school's religious *raison d' etre* will not rise or fall depending on one's own priorities and personality or those of other cultural players.

There is a downside associated with the institutionalization of Catholic culture, however. That is, when Catholic culture is taken for granted or left unattended, the way of life flowing from the culture can grow stagnant and devoid of meaning. Then, within a short period of time, the school's Catholic culture—what once was a vibrant way of life—becomes lifeless and rote.

Recognizing this downside, architects of Catholic culture attend to the continuous renewal of the school's way of life. These women and men view the Catholic school as an "educational project" always "under construction" because they understand that building the Kingdom of God in schools is always a matter of "unfinished business." Again, when the president of a Jesuit high school invoked the Ignatian charism of *magis* in a newspaper advertisement, he spoke directly about this ideal, literally and figuratively, in the uniquely Jesuit "educational project."

Architects of Catholic culture consciously attend to the religious dimension of school life. They audit, appraise, and assess the degree to which Gospel values and religious mission are embedded in the school's culture and way of life. When the stagnating effects of institutionalization are in evidence, architects of Catholic culture initiate programs aimed at cultural renewal or, if necessary, "refound" the school's charism, following the lead of the religious congregations since Vatican II (Arbuckle, 1988).

Norm 6: *As master builders, architects of Catholic culture engage others in the culture building "project."*

Coleman and Hoffer (1987) indicate that strong, cohesive cultures rely on a network of active and supportive adults. This interactive web of adults serves as a vital resource—social capital—essential in the formation of youth.

In light of this research, even though Catholic educational leaders are the primary architects of Catholic culture, they do not build Catholic culture in isolation from the people they lead. These women and men recognize the significance of developing social capital in schools, especially with regard to the faith formation of youth. To achieve this desired outcome, Catholic educational leaders create networks and partnerships among the adult members of the school community. In turn, these networks and partnerships increase the wealth of social capital available for the faith formation of the younger members of the school community.

In essence, architects of Catholic culture capture the Catholic imagination of the school community's adult members. By designing and using cultural building plans that engage these women and men in the continuous process of culture building, architects of Catholic culture light fires within people rather than underneath them.

Norm 7: *Architects of Catholic culture view themselves as God's architects.*

Architects of Catholic culture view themselves as collaborating with God in building the Kingdom of God in Catholic schools. These women and men participate in a long heritage of master builders dating as far back as Jesus' first disciples. Additionally, St. Paul's words "According to the grace of God given to me, like a wise master builder I lay the foundations of faith, and others build on what I have laid" (1 Corinthians 3:10) speak directly to architects of Catholic culture about their lives and work as well as the importance of continuing the mission bequeathed by the first disciples and St. Paul in "laying the foundations of faith," albeit in the context of the Catholic school.

Today's architects of Catholic culture also build upon the heri-

Identify how Norm 6 is evident in your Catholic educational leadership practice:

_____

_____

_____

_____

Cite three actions you will take so that Norm 6 more fully characterizes your Catholic educational leadership practice:

1. _____
2. _____
3. _____

Identify how Norm 7 evidences itself in your Catholic educational leadership practice:

_____

_____

_____

_____

Specify three actions you will take so that Norm 7 is more fully evident in your Catholic educational leadership practice:

1. _____
2. _____
3. _____

tage of those women and men religious and priests who constructed the confederation of American Catholic schools. As heirs to this unique "educational project" (Congregation for Catholic Education, 1997/1998, #4), today's architects of Catholic culture bear the profound responsibility of ensuring that the Catholic school is "a place of integral education of the human person through a clear educational project of which Christ is the foundation" (#4).

As the psalmist declares, "Unless the Lord build the house, they labor in vain who build it" (Psalm 127:1). Thus, architects of Catholic culture discern the Lord's will and look to the Holy Spirit to provide inspiration and guidance in fulfilling their leadership responsibilities. Despite the many deadlines that Catholic educational leaders face and the sense of urgency these women and men oftentimes feel to "get things done yesterday," architects of Catholic culture recognize that "a.s.a.p." also stands for "always say a prayer," finding strength, courage, comfort, and inspiration in Jesus' life and teaching. As the Risen Lord commissioned His disciples to go and teach, He assured the first architects of God's Kingdom, "And behold, I am with you always..." (Matthew 28:20). In this sense, this seventh norm provides the linchpin binding together and summarizing all that precedes for, while architects of Catholic culture view themselves as God's architects, they humbly acknowledge that God is the master builder.

A Concluding Reflection

The Second Vatican Council states that the mission of the Church is "to carry on the work of Christ under the guidance of the Holy Spirit..." (Vatican Council II, 1965d/1996, #3). In turn, each Catholic is called by virtue of the Sacrament of Baptism to carry forward the work of Christ by utilizing one's gifts and talents for the building of God's Kingdom.

God has blessed Catholic educational leaders with a unique and crucial mission, namely, the work and ministry of carrying forward Christ's unfinished mission of building the Kingdom of God in Catholic schools. These women and men are heirs to a rich heritage who bear the privilege of building upon and extending the educational ministry of those disciples who have preceded them. As this generation's architects of Catholic culture contemplate God's call through their baptism, design architectural plans, endeavor to build Catholic culture, and engage the members of their school communities in conversations about these substantive matters, they can stand confident in the knowledge that they are collaborating with God and the other members of the school in building authentic faith communities. In these Catholic schools, students encounter the Risen Lord teaching in their midst and learn to carry forward His work by acting justly, loving tenderly, and walking humbly with their God (Micah 6: 8).

References

Ackerman, R. H., Donaldson, G. A., & van der Bogert, R. (1996). *Making sense as a school leader: Persisting questions, creative opportunities.* San Francisco, CA: Jossey-Bass.

Arbuckle, G. A. (1988). *Out of chaos: Refounding religious congregations.* Mahwah, NJ: Paulist Press.

Argyris, C., & Schön, D. A. (1974). *Theory in practice: Increasing professional effectiveness.* San Francisco: Jossey-Bass.

Arnold, T. W. (1938). *The folklore of capitalism.* New Haven, CT: Yale University Press.

Barnard, C. (1938). *Functions of the executive.* Cambridge, MA: Harvard University Press.

Beck, L. G., & Murphy, J. (1992). Searching for a robust understanding of the principalship. *Educational Administration Quarterly, 28*(3), 387-396.

Bednar, G. J. (1996). *Faith as imagination: The contribution of William F. Lynch, S.J.* Kansas City, MO: Sheed & Ward.

Bellah, R. N., Madsen, R., Sullivan, W. M., Swidler, A., & Tipton, S. M. (1985). *Habits of the heart: Individualism and commitment in American life.* New York: Harper & Row.

Beyer, L. E. (1991). Teacher education, reflective inquiry and moral action. In B. R. Tabachnich & K. M. Zeichner (Eds.), *Issues and practices in inquiry-oriented teacher education* (pp. 113-29). Bristol, PA: The Falmer Press.

Blumberg, A., & Greenfield, W. (1980). *The effective principal: Perspectives on school leadership.* Boston, MA: Allyn and Bacon.

Bolman, L. G., & Deal, T. E. (1997). *Reframing organizations: Artistry, choice, and leadership* (2nd ed.). San Francisco: Jossey-bass.

Bower, M. (1966). *Will to manage.* New York: McGraw Hill.

Boyan, N. J. (1988). *Handbook of research on educational administration.* New York: Longman.

Brandt, R. S. (Ed.). (1997). *What we believe: Positions of the Association for Supervision and Curriculum Development.* Alexandria, VA: Association for Supervision and Curriculum Development.

Brookover, W. B., Beady, C., Flood, P., Schweitzer, J., & Wisenbaker, J. (1979). *School social systems and student achievement: Schools can make a difference.* New York: Praeger.

Brookover, W. B., & Lezotte, L. W. (1979). *Changes in school characteristics coincident with changes in student achievement.* East Lansing, MI: Institute for Research on Teaching, Michigan State University. (ERIC Document Reproduction Service No. ED 181 005)

Brubacher, J. W., Case, C. W., & Reagan, T. G. (1994). *Becoming a reflective educator: How to build a culture of inquiry in the schools.* Thousand Oaks, CA: Corwin Press.

Bryk, A. S., & Driscoll, M. E. (1988). *The high school as community: Contextual influences, and consequences for students and teachers.* Madison, WI: Wisconsin Center for Education Research.

Bryk, A. S., Holland, P. B., Lee, V. E., & Carriedo, R. A. (1984). *Effective Catholic schools: An exploration.* Washington, DC: National Catholic Educational Association.

Bryk, A. S., Lee, V. E., & Holland, P. B. (1993). *Catholic schools and the common good.* Cambridge, MA: Harvard University Press.

Buetow, H. A. (1985). *A history of United States Catholic schooling.* Washington, DC: National Catholic Educational Association.

Chambers, L. (1998). How customer-friendly is your school? *Educational Leadership, 56*(2), 33-35.

Clark, W. C. (1988). The communal charism of education and its application to Catholic high schools in the United States (STD Thesis, Gregorian University, Rome, 1988). *Dissertation Abstracts International, 50-06A,* p. 1702.

Coleman, J.S., Hoffer, T., & Kilgore, S. (1982). *High school achievement: Public, Catholic, and private schools compared.* New York: Basic Books.

Coleman, J. S., & Hoffer, T. (1987). *Public and private high schools: The impact of communities.* New York: Basic Books.

The Commission on Research and Development. (1981/1994). Profile of the graduate of a Jesuit high school at graduation. *Foundations* (pp. 101-106). Washington, DC: Jesuit Secondary Education Association.

Congregation for Catholic Education. (1977). *The Catholic school.* Washington, DC: United States Catholic Conference.

Congregation for Catholic Education. (1982). *Lay Catholics in Schools: Witnesses to faith.* Boston, MA: The Daughters of St. Paul.

Congregation for Catholic Education. (1988). *The Religious dimension of education in a Catholic school.* Washington, DC: United States Catholic Conference.

Congregation for Catholic Education. (1997/1998). The Catholic school on the threshold of the third millennium. In *Catholic Education: A Journal of Inquiry and Practice, 2*(1), 4-14.

Connelly, J. (Ed.). (1976). *A history of the archdiocese of Philadelphia.* Philadelphia, PA: Archdiocese of Philadelphia.

Cook, T. J. (1991). A study of the religious literacy of Catholic high school educators (Doctoral dissertation, Boston College, 1990). *Dissertation Abstracts International, 52-01A,* p. 0123.

Cook, T. J. (1998). Building the kingdom: School leaders as architects of Catholic culture. *Catholic Education: A Journal of Inquiry and Practice, 2*(2), 135.

Cook, T. J. (1999, August/September). Soul searching: What are your school's core values? *Momentum 30*(3), 22-25.

Cook, W. J. (1990). *Strategic planning for America's schools (Rev. ed.).* Arlington, VA: American Association of School Administrators.

Corbettt, D. H., Firestone, W. A., & Rossman, G. B. (1987). Resistance to planned change and the sacred in school culture. *Educational Administration Quarterly, 23*(4), 36-59.

Culbertson, J. A. (1988). A century's quest for a knowledge base. In N. J. Boyan (Ed.), *Handbook of research on educational administration* (pp. 3-26). White Plains, NY: Longman, Inc.

Cusick, P. A. (1992). *The educational system: Its nature and logic.* New York: McGraw-Hill.

Cutler, W. W., III. (1989). Cathedral of culture: The schoolhouse in American educational thought and practice since 1820. *History of Education Quarterly, 29*(1), 1-40.

Davis, R. C., & Schleifer, R. (1994). *Contemporary literary criticism: Literary and cultural studies* (3rd ed.). New York: Longman.

Deal, T. E. (1985). The symbolism of effective school. *The Elementary School Journal, 85*(5), 601-620.

Deal, T. E. (1991). Private schools: Bridging Mr. Chips and my captain. *Teachers College Record 92*(3), 415 424.

Deal, T. E. (1993). The culture of schools. In M. Sashkin & H. J. Walberg (Eds.), *Educational leadership and school culture* (pp. 3-18). Berkeley, CA: McCutchan.

Deal, T. E., & Kennedy, A. A. (1982). *Corporate cultures: The rites and rituals of corporate life.* Reading, MA: Addison-Wesley.

Deal, T. E., & Peterson, K.D. (1990). *The principal's role in shaping school culture.* Washington, DC: U.S. Government Printing Office.

Deal, T. E., & Peterson, K. D. (1999). *Shaping school culture: The heart of leadership.* San Francisco: Jossey-Bass.

Dewey, J. (1910). *How we think.* Boston: D.C. Heath & Company.

Dolan, J. P. (1985). *The American Catholic experience: A history from colonial times to the present.* New York: Doubleday.

Dulles, A. (1988). *The reshaping of Catholicism: Current challenges in the theology of church.* San Francisco: Harper & Row.

Effective Instructional Management. (1983). Arlington, VA: Association for Supervision and Curriculum Development.

Ellett, C. D. (1992). Principal evaluation and assessment. In M. Alkins (Ed.), *Encyclopedia of educational research* (6th ed, pp. 1026-1031). Los Angeles, CA: MacMillan Publishing Company.

Finke, R., & Stark, R. (1992). *The churching of America, 1776-1990: Winners and losers in our religious economy.* New Brunswick, NJ: Rutgers University Press.

Fitzpatrick, J. P. (1987). *One church, many cultures: The challenge of diversity.* Kansas City, MO: Sheed & Ward.

Flynn, M. (1993). *The culture of Catholic schools.* Homebush, NSW, Australia: St. Paul.

Foster, W. P. (1980a). The changing administrator: Developing managerial praxis. *Educational Theory, 30*(1), 11-23.

Foster, W. P. (1980a). Administration and the crisis in legitimacy: A review of Habermasian thought. *Harvard Educational Review, 50*(4), 496-505.

Fowler, W. J., Jr. (1991). *What are the characteristics of principals viewed as effective by teachers?* (ERIC ED 347 675). Eugene, OR: ERIC Clearinghouse on Educational Management.

Fullan, M. (1993). *Change forces: Probing the depths of educational reform.* Bristol, PA: Falmer Press.

Fullan, M. (1997). *What's worth fighting for in the principalship?* New York: Teacher's College Press.

Galetto, P. W. (1996). *Building the foundations of faith: The religious knowledge, beliefs, and practices of Catholic elementary school teachers of religion.* Washington, DC: National Catholic Educational Association.

Gallup, G. Jr., & Castelli, J. (1987). *The American Catholic people: Their beliefs, practices, and values.* New York: Doubleday.

Gardner, H. (1995). *Leading Minds: An anatomy of leadership.* New York: Basic Books.

Getzels, J. W., & Guba, E. G. (1957). Social behavior and the administrative process. *The School Review, 29*, 30-40.

Gilkey, L. (1975). *Catholicism confronts modernity: A Protestant view.* New York: Seabury Press.

Goldman, P., & Kempner, K. (1988). *The administrators view of professional training* (ERIC ED 325 979). Eugene, OR: ERIC Clearinghouse on Educational Management.

Grant, G. (1981). The character of education and the education of character. *Daedalus, 110*, 135-149.

Grant, G. (1982, March). The elements of a strong positive ethos. *NA-ASP Bulletin, 66*(452), 84-90.

Grant, G. (1985). Schools that make an imprint: Creating a strong positive ethos. In J. H. Bunzel (Ed.), *Challenge to American schools: The case for standards and values*. New York: Oxford University Press.

Greeley, A. M. (1985). *American Catholics since the council: An unauthorized report*. Chicago: Thomas More.

Greeley, A. M. (1990). *The Catholic myth: The behavior and beliefs of American Catholics*. New York: Charles Scribner's Sons.

Greeley, A. M. (1995). Why do Catholics stay in the church? *U.S. Catholic, 60*, 31-35.

Greeley, A. M. (2000). *The Catholic imagination*. Berkeley, CA: University of California Press.

Greeley, A. M., McCready, W.C., & McCourt, K. (1976). *Catholic schools in a declining church*. Kansas City, MO: Sheed & Ward.

Griffiths, D. E. (1988). Administrative theory. In N. Boyan (Ed.), *Handbook of research on educational administration* (pp. 27-51). New York: Longman.

Groome, T. (1996). What makes a school Catholic? In T. McLaughlin, J. O'Keefe, & B. O'Keefe (Eds.), *The contemporary Catholic school: Context, identity and diversity* (pp. 107-125). Washington, DC: Falmer Press.

Groome, T. (1998). *Educating for life: A spiritual vision for every teacher and parent*. Allen, TX: Thomas More.

Hemphill, J. K., Griffiths, D. E., & Fredriksen, N. (1962). *Administrative performance and personality*. New York: Teachers College Press.

Hellwig, M. (1995, Fall). The best of times, the worst of times: Catholic intellectual life in today's academic setting. *Conversations, 8*, 15-19.

Hilton, M. E. (1997). *Sharing the spirit: Transmission of charism by religious congregations*. Unpublished doctoral dissertation, University of Melbourne, Victoria, Australia.

Hughes, L. W. (Ed.). (1999). *The principal as leader* (2nd ed.). Upper Saddle River, NY: Prentice Hall.

Jackall, R. (1988). *Moral mazes*. New York: Oxford University Press.

Jacobs, R. M. (1996). *The vocation of the Catholic educator*. Washington, DC: National Catholic Educational Association.

Jacobs, R. M. (1997). *The grammar of Catholic schooling*. Washington, DC: National Catholic Educational Association.

Jacobs, R. M. (1998a). U.S. Catholic schools and the religious who served in them: Contributions in the 18th and 19th centuries. *Catholic Education: A Journal of Inquiry and Practice, 1*(4), 364-383.

Jacobs, R. M. (1998b). U.S. Catholic schools and the religious who served in them: Contributions in the first six decades of the 20th century. *Catholic Education: A Journal of Inquiry and Practice, 2*(1), 15-34.

Jacobs, R. M. (1998c). U.S. Catholic schools and the religious who served in them: The struggle to continue the tradition in the post-Vatican II era. *Catholic Education: A Journal of Inquiry and Practice, 2*(2), 159-176.

Johnston, J. H. (1987, March). Values, culture, and the effective school. *NASSP Bulletin 71*(497), 79-88.

Johnston, J. H. (1995, November/December). Climate: Building a culture of achievement. *Schools in the Middle, 5*(2), 10-15.

Kealey, R. J. (1987). *The prayer of Catholic educators*. Washington, DC: National Catholic Educational Association.

Keller, J. D. (1999). Deciphering teacher lounge talk. *Phi Delta Kappan, 81*(4), 328-329.

Lakoff, G., & Johnson, M. (1980). *Metaphors we live by*. Chicago: The University of Chicago Press.

Lambert, L. (1998). *Building leadership capacity in schools*. Alexandria, VA: Association for Supervision and Curriculum Development.

Lightfoot, S. L. (1983). *The good high school: Portraits of character and culture*. New York: Basic Books.

Maehr, M. L., & Buck, R. M. (1993). Transforming school culture. In M. Sashkin & H. J. Walberg (Eds.), *Educational leadership and school culture* (pp. 40-57). Berkeley, CA: McCutchan.

Maritain, J. (1943). *Education at the crossroads*. New Haven, CN: Yale University Press.

Maslow, A. H. (1970). *Motivation and personality*. New York: Harper & Row.

McBride, A. A. (1983). *Interviewing and supporting the Catholic educator*. Washington, DC: National Catholic Educational Association.

McBrien, R. P. (1994). *Catholicism: New edition*. San Francisco: HarperCollins.

McDermott, E. J. (1997). *Distinctive qualities of the Catholic school* (2nd ed.). Washington, DC: National Catholic Educational Association.

McDonald, D. (2000). *United States Catholic elementary and secondary schools 1999-2000*. Washington, DC: National Catholic Educational Association.

McDonough, E. (1993, September-October). Charisms and religious life. *Review for Religious, 52*(5), 646-659.

Murphy, J. (1990). Principal instructional leadership. In P. W. Thurston & L. S. Lotto (Eds.), *Perspectives on the school: Advances in educational administration* (Volume 1, Part B, 163-200). Greenwich, CN: JAI Press Inc.

Murphy, J. (1992). *The landscape of leadership preparation: Reframing the education of school administrators.* Newbury Park, CA: Corwin Press, Inc.

Murphy, J., & Louis, K. S. (1999). *Handbook of research on educational administration* (2nd ed.). Washington, DC: American Educational Research Association.

Nardoni, E. (1993). The concept of charism in Paul. *The Catholic Biblical Quarterly, 55*, 68-80.

National Conference of Catholic Bishops. (1972). *To teach as Jesus did.* Washington, DC: United States Catholic Conference.

National Conference of Catholic Bishops. (1976). *Teach them.* Washington, DC: United States Catholic Conference.

National Conference of Catholic Bishops. (1979). *Sharing the light of faith: National catechetical directory for Catholics of the United States.* Washington, DC: United States Catholic Conference.

National Conference of Catholic Bishops. (1993). *Stewardship: A disciple's response.* Washington, DC: United States Catholic Conference.

National Congress on Catholic Schools for the 21st Century. (1992). *Executive summary.* Washington, DC: National Catholic Educational Association.

New England Association of Schools and Colleges. (1994). The culture/identity of the school. In *Manual for school evaluation* (7th ed., pp. 61-62). Bedford, MA: Author.

Newton, R. R. (1979). A systematic approach to faculty religious development. *The Living Light, 16*, 328-341.

Omaha World-Herald. (2000, March 11).

O'Malley, W. J. (1991). Evangelizing the unconverted. In F. D. Kelly (Ed.), *What makes a school Catholic?* (pp. 3-9). Washington, DC: National Catholic Educational Association.

Peters, T. J., & Waterman, R. H., Jr. (1982). *In search of excellence.* New York: Warner.

Prestine, N. A., & Thurston, P. W. (Eds.). (1994). New directions in educational administration: Policy, preparation, and practice. *Advances in educational administration* (Volume 3). Greenwich, CN: JAI Press Inc.

Purkey, S. C., & Smith, M. S. (1982, December). Too soon to cheer? Synthesis of research on effective schools. *Educational Leadership, 40*(3), 64-69.

Purkey, S. C., & Smith, M. S. (1983). Effective schools: A review. *Elementary School Journal, 83*(4) 427-452.

Purkey, S. C., & Smith, M. S. (1985). Educational policy and school effectiveness. In G. R. Austin & H. Garber (Eds.), *Research on exemplary schools* (pp. 181-200). New York: Academic Press.

Reck, C. (1983). *Vision and values*. Washington, DC: National Catholic Educational Association.

Renfro, J. M. (1986). Religious charism: Definition, rediscovery and implications. *Review for Religious, 45*(4), 520-530.

Rutter, M., Maughan, B., Mortimore, P., Ouston, J., & Smith, A. (1979). *Fifteen thousand hours: Secondary schools and their effects on children*. Cambridge, MA: Harvard University Press.

Ryan, K., & Cooper, J. M. (1995*). Those who can, teach* (7th ed.) Boston, MA: Houghton Mifflin.

Saints and feast days. (1985). Chicago: Loyola University Press.

Schein, E. H. (1992). *Organizational culture and leadership* (2nd ed.). San Francisco: Jossey-Bass.

Schnur, S. I. (1989). *The training of educational administrators: Perceptions of building principals*. Unpublished doctoral dissertation, Fordham University.

Schön, D. A. (1991). *Educating the reflective practitioner*. San Francisco: Jossey-Bass.

Schuttloffel, M. J. (1999). *Character and the contemplative principal*. Washington, DC: National Catholic Educational Association.

Selznick, P. (1957). *Leadership and administration*. New York: Harper & Row.

Sergiovanni, T. J. (1984, February). Leadership and excellence in schooling. *Educational Leadership, 41*(5), 4-13.

Sergiovanni, T. J. (1986). Understanding reflective practice. *Journal of Curriculum and Supervision, 1*(4), 353-359.

Sergiovanni, T. J. (1994a). Organizations or communities? Changing the metaphor changes the theory. *Educational Administration Quarterly, 30*(2, May), 214-226.

Sergiovanni, T. J. (1994b). *Building community in schools*. San Francisco: Jossey-Bass.

Sergiovanni, T. J. (1995a). *The principalship: A reflective practice perspective* (3rd ed.). Needham Heights, MA: Allyn and Bacon.

Sergiovanni, T. J. (1995b). *Leadership for the schoolhouse: How is it different? Why is it important?* San Francisco: Jossey-Bass.

Sergiovanni, T. J., & Corbally, J. E. (1984). *Leadership and organizational culture.* Chicago: University of Illinois Press.

Simon, H. A. (1945/1997). *Administrative behavior: A study of decision-making processes in administrative organizations.* New York: The Free Press.

Smith, S. C., & Piele, P. K. (Eds.). (1989). *School leadership: Handbook for excellence* (2nd ed.). Eugene, OR: ERIC Clearinghouse on Educational Management.

Smylie, M. A., & Brownlee-Conyers, J. (1992). Teacher leaders and their principals: Exploring the development of new working relationships. *Educational Administration Quarterly, 28*(2), 150-184.

Teddlie, C. (1994). The study of context in school effects research: History, methods, results, and theoretical implications. In D. Reynolds, B. Creemers, P. Nesselrodt, E. Schaffer, S. Stringfield, & C. Teddlie (Eds.), *Advances in school effectiveness research and practice* (pp. 85-110). Tarrytown, NY: Pergamon.

Thomson, S. D. (Ed.). (1992). *School leadership.* Newbury Park, CA: Corwin Press, Inc.

Thomson, S. D. (Ed.). (1993). *Principals for our changing schools: The knowledge and skill base.* Fairfax, VA: National Policy Board for Educational Administration.

Tichy, N. M., & Devanna, M. A. (1986). *The transformational leader.* New York: John Wiley & Sons.

Tracy, D. (1981). *The analogical imagination.* New York: Crossroad.

Trambley, A. (1989, Summer). Getting the question right. *Pax Christi USA Magazine, XIV*(2), 33.

Trice, H. M., & Beyer, J. M. (1993). *The cultures of work organizations.* Englewood Cliffs, NJ: Prentice Hall.

Tyack, D., & Tobin, W. (1994). The "grammar" of schooling: Why has it been so hard to change? *American Educational Research Journal, 31*(3), 452-479.

Vaill, P. B. (1986). The purposing of high-performing systems. In T. J. Sergiovanni & J. E. Corbally (Eds.), *Leadership and organizational culture* (pp. 89-104). Urbana, IL: University of Illinois Press.

Vatican Council II. (1965a/1996). Declaration on Christian education (*Gravissimum Educationis*). In A. Flannery (Ed.), *Vatican Council II: The basic sixteen documents* (pp. 575-591). Northport, NY: Costello Publishing Co.

Vatican Council II. (1965b/1996). Decree on the apostolate of lay people (*Apostolicam actuositatem*). In A. Flannery (Ed.), *Vatican Council II: The basic sixteen documents* (pp. 403-442). Northport, NY: Costello Publishing Co.

Vatican Council II. (1965c/1996). Dogmatic constitution on the Church (*Lumen Gentium*). In A. Flannery (Ed.), *Vatican Council II: The basic sixteen documents* (pp.1-95). Northport, NY: Costello Publishing Co.

Vatican Council II. (1965d/1996). Pastoral Constitution on the Church in the modern world (*Gaudium et Spes*). In A. Flannery (Ed.), *Vatican Council II: The basic sixteen documents* (pp. 163-282). Northport, NY: Costello Publishing Co.

Walch, T. (1996). *Parish school: American Catholic parochial education from colonial times to the present.* New York: Crossroad.

Wildman, L. (1991). *Does the doctorate make a difference?* (ERIC ED 336 827). Eugene, OR: ERIC Clearinghouse on Educational Management.

Wolgast, E. (1992). *Ethics of an artificial person: Lost responsibility in professions and organizations.* Stanford, CA: Stanford University Press.

Zappulla, E. (1983). *Evaluating administative performance: Cultural trends and techniques.* Belmont, CA: Star Publishing Company.